Integration Testing from the Trenches

Nicolas Fränkel

Integration Testing from the Trenches

Nicolas Fränkel

This book is for sale at https://leanpub.com/integrationtest/

This version was published on 2015-02-19

ISBN 978-2955021439

Leanpub

This is a Leanpub book. Leanpub empowers authors and publishers with the Lean Publishing process. Lean Publishing is the act of publishing an in-progress ebook using lightweight tools and many iterations to get reader feedback, pivot until you have the right book and build traction once you do.

Tweet This Book!

Please help Nicolas Fränkel by spreading the word about this book on Twitter!

The suggested tweet for this book is:

Read "Integration Testing from the Trenches", have a look at it https://leanpub.com/integrationtest #integrationtesting #testing

The suggested hashtag for this book is #integrationtesting.

Find out what other people are saying about the book by clicking on this link to search for this hashtag on Twitter:

https://twitter.com/search?q=#integrationtesting

Contents

Foreword by Aslak Knutsen

For the last decade or so there has been an increased focus on Test Driven Development. Surprisingly, the practices described as Test Driven Development dates back to the early 60's.

As new generations of developers sprung up, the practice of Test Driven Development got lost.

A short sighted tendency to produce production code as fast as possible became the norm. There are many factors to why this happened and it's not entirely the developers fault. Somewhere along the line testing became an after thought. The ownership of testing shifted. We handed over the responsibility to another team or department.

Unfortunately, the makers of libraries, frameworks and products suffer from the same "testing as an after thought" short sightedness. As users of their tools, we are often left to fend for ourselves and decipher how to verify our usage. This does not improve our ability to perform Test Driven Development.

This leads to a situation where we're forced to mock, fake and wiggle our way around these frameworks. The result is limiting the testing focusing only on our own code. While in reality it's extremely seldom our own code is the only code involved. "Let's leave all the difficult parts to the integration testing level." In practice the integration testing level is non existent.

In the mist of a hectic project it's easy to forget that while it may simplify *your* day in the short run, your *users* actually live on the 'integration/system' testing level, not the unit level. If it doesn't work on the integration level; it doesn't work. Regardless of what the unit level might portray.

We need to get back to our roots:

Testing *is* development.

Integration Testing from the Trenches doesn't just guide you through some light theory on how you can improve your code to make it more test efficient, but also dives into the harder parts to show you tools that can help you lure out bugs from the darkest corners and from multiple different angles. REST, SOAP, JMS, SMTP, FTP and Databases can all be put to the test with a little help from your new testing friends.

On your next journey don't travel alone, bring your new found testing friends with you.

Happy reading!

Aslak Knutsen,
Arquillian Project Lead, Senior Software Engineer at Red Hat

Foreword by Josh Long - Unit Testing in a Distributed World

I leapt at the chance to read this book and I was even more pleased when Nicolas asked me to pen a foreword for it. It is a very prescient introduction to integration testing for modern applications and services. It could not have come at a better time for Spring and for those looking to build modern applications. It will be my go-to response for the numerous questions surrounding integration testing that I get in my capacity as the Spring Developer Advocate at Pivotal. If you needed the endorsement and want to dive straight away into the text, then there you have it, I won't stop you!

If you're still here, let me tell you about Nicolas, and why this book will always be an important addition to my personal bookshelf.

I serve the Spring community, one that is millions strong and worldwide. Among other things, I have the privilege of putting together a roundup every Tuesday called *This Week in Spring* that aggregates all sorts of awesome content - often from the community - about Spring and peripheral ecosystem technologies like Cloud Foundry, RabbitMQ, Apache Hadoop, Redis, Neo4j, Vaadin, and many others besides. Nicolas is one of the rare technologists whose interests intersect many different communities (like Spring and Vaadin) and he regularly puts together good content that ends up in the roundup. (Thank you, Nicolas!)

I spend a lot of time talking to developers about how to build modern applications and services with Spring. Applications today are increasingly built as *microservices*. This style offers many benefits, particularly when paired with the dynamics of cloud computing. In order to build a microservice-style architecture, functionality is teased apart into small, singly focused services exposed over the network. A service built this way can be evolved independant of other services, free to choose their own technology stacks and deployment schedules.

This approach does introduce some problems. Spring Boot (and other technologies like DropWizard) make it trivial to standup a REST service, but this is still slightly more involved than just invoking methods on `java.lang.Objects`. There is inherent complexity involved in invoking distributed, networked services, and Spring Cloud can alleviate much of this. In this paradigm, it is critical to maintain a stable interface between network services. Where the compiler caught breaks in the interfaces between modules for us before, we must rely on rigorous inter-service testing to ensure stability. Where unit tests verified the interactions between objects for us before, we must rely on *integration tests*.

Unit tests and integration tests are hard to do correctly. Spring provides a expansive toolbox to support testing, and Nicolas does an amazing job explaining it. This book also provides practical, integration-centric approaches to testing all manner of things *beyond* Spring. Things that are *not* built from the ground up to be testable, like Java EE container services, REST, SOAP, FTP, and file systems.

I hope you'll read this book and internalize it. The more you can do to remove the fear involved in integration, the more effectively you'll be able to build applications that exploit modern cloud platforms and deliver faster, more scaleable applications.

Josh Long
@starbuxman
Spring Developer Advocate, Pivotal
San Francisco, CA - February 2015

Preface

I've always been fascinated by Testing. That's strange, but true. Not the manual, boring and repetitive testing but the automated kind, where the result is either a green bar or a BUILD SUCCESS message. Just typing a command-line and knowing the computer will check the correctness of your code is very satisfying for me. And of course, when tools computing code coverage were made available for the masses (read *free*), I competed in the race for a higher code coverage - such is the power of gamification.

However, despite aiming and achieving for high code coverage, I couldn't stop noticing that there were bugs that were not caught by my test harness. Most of those bugs did not happen in my unit tests, because they were not coming from the behavior of a single class, but they sparked from the collaboration of multiple classes. Good unit tests focus on a *unit*, and we've been taught in the Java world that a unit means a class. That is the reason why we mock dependencies: to test a single class in isolation.

Besides, some classes couldn't be unit tested. Of course Data Acess Objects come to mind but basically also every class that interacted with an outside dependency, be it a database or a web service. And though databases had always been there, web service dependencies were becoming more and more common. Of course, I could deploy the application and test it manually (and I do), but nothing beats the feeling of safety that one has with an automated test harness. So I went on to create tests that verified the collaborations of classes, tests that checked the correct behavior of classes interacting with outside dependencies and also tests that simulated users through the Graphical User Interface. Not only did I spend much time developing this, I also noticed some of the tests regularly failed, because of some environment instability. Of course, those tests were quickly removed from the build, because a sentinel that always warns you about a danger, regardless of the reality, is no better than no sentinel at all.

Meanwhile, the whole Unit Testing - and Test-Driven-Development to a lesser extent, has become the bread and butter of software engineers around the globe while Integration Testing seems sometimes at best misused and at worst completely ignored. There are some initiatives that go into the right direction, such as Spring MVC Test and Arquillian for Java EE.

The good thing with Unit Testing is that it's quite easy to understand, to set up and to use. This is not the case with Integration Testing as you are testing collaboration of components inside the application or integration with dependencies outside the application. Thus, the game of Integration Testing is more like a trial-and-failure kind of process. I've tried and I've failed and I've done that many times, each time coming closer to my target: deliver better software quality and more robust applications to end-users with a reasonable cost. This book is about what I've learned by doing so. Don't worry, you'll do your own mistakes! But I'll consider my goal fulfilled if I could spare you some time in the process.

Have a nice trip on the path of Integration Testing!

About the author

Nicolas Frankel operates as a successful Java and Java EE Software Architect and Developer with more than a decade of experience in consulting for many different customers, in a wide range of contexts (such as telecoms, banking, insurances, large retail and public sector). Nicolas's interests in software are broad, ranging from Rich Client Application, to open source software in general, and include build automation, Quality Processes as well as diverse flavors of testing.

He's currently employed by an eCommerce solution vendor leader and does consulting for a Blue Chip company. He also doubles as a teacher in universities and higher education schools and a trainer for experienced pros - he also obviously triples as a book author.

In his free time, he may be found practicing sports: running, squashing and skiing at the moment. Other leisure activities include reading novels, motorcycling, photography and drawing, not necessarily in that order.

About the reviewers

Eddy Cingala is a Senior Java Developer and a Scrum Master. He likes to apply engineering principles to software development. This include technical disciplines and agile processes. He likes to develop and work with well structured code, that can evolve. This is one of his motivation for being a reviewer of this book on Integration Testing.

With more than 10 years of experience, he also deploys agile processes during the projects he works on. He also organises some events related to Scrum, like the Geneva Scrum Beer. He graduated from Telecom Saint-Etienne Engineering school.

When not busy at work, he practices badminton and many activities related to electronic music compos.

John Barrow is a consultant working for hybris software, helping enterprise customers make the most of their investment in the market-leading e-commerce platform. He has more than 15 years experience in the IT industry, having previously worked as a Technical Architect for one of the big four accountancy firms, and as CTO for a startup developing software for the automotive industry. He has also co-authored 2 IBM Redbooks. When not working, he enjoys swimming and spending time (and money) with his wife, and dreaming of driving around the south of France in a renovated Citroen HY van.

Book structure

This book is organized along the following lines:

- *Chapter 1 - Foundations of testing* is an introductory chapter, laying out the foundations for the rest of the book. It describes Unit Testing, Integration Testing and Functional Testing, as well as their associated notions.
- *Chapter 2 - Developer testing tools* covers both the JUnit and TestNG testing frameworks. Tips and tricks on how to use them for Integration Testing are also included.
- *Chapter 3 - Test-Friendly Design* details Dependency Injection, DI-compatible design and which objects should be set as dependencies during tests execution. This includes definitions of Test Doubles, such as Dummy, Fake and Mock along with an explanation of Mockito, a Mocking framework and Spring Test and Mockrunner, two Fake libraries.
- *Chapter 4 - Automated testing* covers how to get our carefully crafted Integration Tests inside automated building processes, whether they run locally or on a remote server.
- *Chapter 5 - Testing Integration with Infrastructure Resources* concerns itself about testing applications that need infrastructure resources such as databases, mail servers, ftp servers and others. Tools and techniques about each resource type will be explained.
- *Chapter 6 - Testing Integration with Web Services* is solely dedicated to testing applications that require Web Services, either in SOAP or REST flavor.
- In *Chapter 7 - Spring in-container testing*, testing recipes for Spring applications are described. This includes coverage of the Spring Test library, as well as the Springockito utility.
- *Chapter 8 - Spring Web MVC testing* details how to test Spring MVC applications. This includes specific areas of Spring Test regarding Mock MVC to test from the URL layer.
- *Chapter 9 - Java EE testing* covers testing of Java EE applications, including the Arquillian testing framework.

1. Foundations of testing

This chapter is the introduction to the book and is the opportunity to have a look at some definitions in the testing domain:

- Testing in general
- Unit Testing, its characteristics and limitations
- Integration Testing, its characteristics and disadvantages
- Other testing flavors

1.1 Defining testing

Testing is a very rich domain, perhaps as old as programming itself. How can a developer be sure their program behaves as expected if he/she does not test it first? In this regard, a very generic testing definition can be provided:

 Testing

In software, testing is the process that checks that a running software system - or piece(s) thereof, conforms to expected results when provided with known input.

Note that this definition covers nearly every testing process found, from software created by a student in his parent's garage to enterprise-grade software costing billions. To provide this definition, some variables are conveniently left out:

What

It does not define what expected results are made of; they could be formal written requirements or just a quick oral request from the boss

Who

> It does not define which actor is responsible for the testing. It might be the developer himself, the business analyst who wrote down the specifications, or a dedicated tester in the Quality Assurance team

How

> It does not define the process used to execute the check: this could range from the simplest method - run the application, fill in fields and submit, to the most automated system, complete with traceability back to the specifications

1.1.1 System Under Test

Defining the part of the system is of utmost importance.

> *The "system under test". It is short for "whatever thing we are testing" and is always defined from the perspective of the test. When we are writing unit tests the system under test (SUT) is whatever class (a.k.a. CUT), object (a.k.a. OUT) or method(s) (a.k.a. MUT) we are testing; when we are writing customer tests, the SUT is probably the entire application (a.k.a. AUT) or at least a major subsystem of it. The parts of the application that we are not verifying in this particular test may still be involved as a depended-on component (DOC).*

Source: http://xunitpatterns.com/SUT.html

 # System Under Test

The System Under Test describes the boundaries of the System in regard to the outside

This defines what is provided and known as opposed to what is to be tested. In other words, the SUT defines the limits of the tested system.

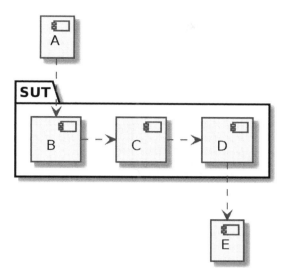

Fig. 1.1 - Simplified System Under Test modeling

In the previous diagram, the SUT is made of components B, C and D. Collaboration between those components is to be tested, while component A calls component B with parameters necessary to cover the required test cases. Component E also stands outside the SUT.

It is of course possible to logically decompose a system into different subsystems, each one becoming a SUT for a test suite. Those SUT may:

- Have different granularities, some being comprised of only a few classes, some encompassing almost the whole system
- Overlap, some test suites require the use of the same components

1.1.2 Repeatable results

Whatever the specifics, the following are mandatory in any standard testing process:

1. The SUT, of course
2. A known input
3. An expected result

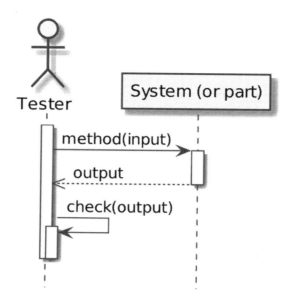

Fig. 1.2 - Testing, input and output

Note that for the last point, the result is expected to be the same over and over provided both system and result(s) are invariants: determinism is needed so that repeated testing of the system will always yield the same *OK* or *KO* result.

This statement may seem obvious, but some software development domains are border case in this regard. Arithmetic is a good example of the former case: take the add(int,int) method and 1 and 1 as input parameters, the expected result would be 2 (in base 10).

On the oppoiste, games of chance will be hard to test if a set result is needed. A results range will probably need to be tested , but the randomness itself has to be checked as well. For example, for a simple 6-sided dice roll, the result should be between 1 and 6 **and** the specific result probability should be 1/6 given a large enough sample.

Once we have repeatable results, we can make sure all tests pass before any change in our code base. Therefore, any test that does not pass after that points to a potential problem in our software. On the contrary, passing all tests before and after a code base change gives a high degree of confidence that there is no regression.

1.1.3 Assertions, errors and failures

Let us first define some terms.

Assertion

During test execution, assertion is the check that *specifies* whether the test passes (or not).

Tests may end up in error for one of these two reasons:

- During assertion, results were not those that were expected, *e.g.* `true` was asserted but the result was `false` (or the other way around).
- Somewhere during test execution, something unexpected happens. It may be an `Exception`, but not necessarily as exceptions may be expected like any other test results.

Failure vs. error

Failures happen when assertions fail *e.g* a test expected `true` but the returned result was `false`, or it expected a thrown exception but nothing of the sort happened. They are the reason tests are made in the first place, to ensure code still behave as expected regardless of changes. Failures are expectations not met.

Errors happen when something goes so wrong the testing code is not able to handle it *e.g.* when an **unexpected** exception is thrown. Errors are unexpected and point to a testing code not robust enough.

1.2 Unit Testing

While it may seem somewhat strange to provide a section about Unit Testing (https://en.wikipedia.org/wiki/Unit_testing) in a book on Integration Testing, the former has some a very strong influence on the latter. In particular, as will be seen later, one may define the other. Moreover, some techniques used with Unit Testing can also successfully be used in Integration Testing. Even among some seasoned developers, it seems Unit Testing definition is fuzzy - at best.

> Some have tried to argue that since they used the JUnit framework, they were Unit Testing. Of course, this is not a way to define Unit Testing.

For a relevant definition, the most general way to describe Unit Testing is the following:

 Unit Testing

Unit Testing is a strategy to test a *unit of code* in *isolation*.

Notice two important terms:

Isolation

Isolation means the unit should be tested independently of all other units.

Unit of code

The real hardship comes from defining the unit to be tested. In Object-Oriented Programming languages in general and the Java world in particular, there are several levels of granularity that may fill this role:

- Method
- Class
- Package

- JAR
- WAR
- EAR
- etc.

Any of those would make fine units. However, the current agreement in the software community is that the method - the most fine-grained unit of all, is the unit to test. Therefore, our former definition should be amended as follows:

 ## Unit Testing

Unit Testing is a strategy to test *methods in isolation*.

A way to achieve this will be described in *Chapter 3*. The point is, **if code is not tested in isolation at the method level, it is not unit tested**, though it does not mean it is not tested.

As an example, let us consider a basic Java class:

Code 1.1 - A simple class to test

```
1  public class Calculus {
2      public int add(int a, int b) {
3          return a + b;
4      }
5  }
```

Obviously, the add() method computes the addition of two int and returns the result. It can be easily tested in isolation, and as such is a very good candidate for a unit test. Considering our previous stance on determinism, the parts can be mapped are the following:

Code to unit test	The add() method
Known input	1 and 1
Expected result	2

Another important feature of Unit Testing - but also of most forms of testing - is to ensure automation: tests should be run by the click of a button or by a command line instruction, but they must not require more human interaction. In some cases, it requires even less, as in the case of Continuous Integration: more details can be found in *Chapter 4 - Automated testing*, entirely dedicated to Automated Testing.

1.2.1 Why unit test?

Unit Testing code let us be quietly confident in our software's atomic components *i.e* methods. Taking a car assembly as a comparison, Unit Testing is making sure every part used in a car is fit enough to do its job once the car is fully assembled.

In this context, a windshield can be unit tested for shocks, by throwing calibrated stones at it and asserting that it does not break (the glass it is made of can crack though). It does not mean it will fit the car perfectly: this is outside the realm of Unit Testing. Likewise, a tire can be tested to check it deflates in a *safe* way when punctured. To test the tire's adherence to the road when faced with some depth of water requires the collaboration of the other 3 wheels and their respective shocks so it goes beyond Unit Testing.

In software development, Unit Testing targets both code design and quality. It also allows us to cover corner cases, *e.g* dividing by zero and the like.

1.2.2 Unit Testing enablement

Traditional software development good practices emphasizes modularity: although true in general, it is of the essence of successful Object-Oriented Programming languages. This creates dependencies between an application's components, they need to work together to achieve some result. Each system component has a distinct responsibility in the collaboration.

For example, an e-commerce application will have dedicated components:

- An list of items to put in the cart
- A cart to hold these items
- A checkout process to buy them

- etc.

This is desirable from a maintenance point of view, as when a feature is needed or when a bug is detected, it is generally easy to locate where to implement this feature or where to fix this bug. It becomes less desirable from a testing point of view, as code has to be tested in isolation. Hence, dependencies are a big hindrance to that.

Chapter 3 - Test-Friendly Design will describe how to benefit from modularization while enabling Unit Testing.

1.2.3 Testing private methods

Most literature frowns upon testing private methods; they are in fact private and thus subject to change. Providing tests for private methods would mean those tests would probably have to be changed each time methods themselves changed. Instead, it is recommended to test only the public API as it is much more stable.

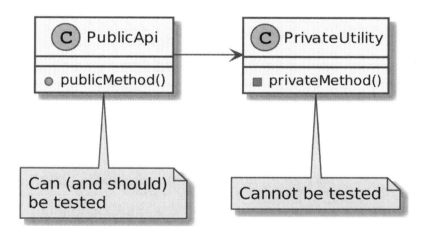

Fig. 1.3 - Testing the public API

However, one should strive to follow a pragmatic approach - definitely a recurring theme in this book.

Therefore, if the context mandates testing a private method, it is just a matter of changing the `private` modifier to a default package one. This way, testing the *formerly-private-now-package* method is just a matter of creating a class in the same package to test it.

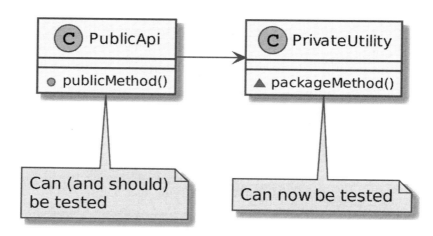

Fig. 1.4 - Testing private methods

1.2.4 Unit Testing requirements

Unit Testing also has unique requirements in regards to other kinds of testing.

Isolated

    Let's write it once more - it does not hurt: Unit Testing tests a method **in isolation,** meaning it has to be tested independently of any other piece of code. This may be achieved by the Dependency Injection design technique described in *Chapter 3 - Test-Friendly Design.*

Fast   Unit Testing is our first safety net, before all other kinds of test. Therefore, it is mandatory that those tests be blazingly fast, so fast that unit test execution time should be measured in milliseconds, not in seconds. The good thing is that if tests are isolated as written in the previous section, they will be this fast. As a corollary, if they are not, external dependencies should probably be checked for and then removed to provide proper isolation.

Complete

    An often overlooked requirement for unit tests is that they should provide high completeness, proved by a high code coverage. In this regard, Unit Testing should not only test for standard behavior - the "happy path", but also border cases and error-handling cases.

1.2.5 Level of detail

Unit Testing is a mandatory process in software development. Yet it cannot ensure the final software will meet all requirements, for its responsibility is to test components in isolation, ensuring each and every piece of code works well by itself.

Thus, Unit Testing will not detect bugs introduced by two components collaborating to achieve a result.

Using the car example, each single car piece can be tested for defects, but that does not mean the car itself will perform correctly. As was seen previously with the windshield and tire examples, assembly of those pieces - up to the whole car itself, also has to be tested for defects.

1.3 Integration Testing

At this point, testing and Unit Testing have been defined. It is now time to give our attention to the core subject of this book. In comparison to Unit Testing, defining Integration Testing is very simple. When testing goes beyond Unit Testing, it becomes an integration test. Or to put it in other words:

 Integration Testing

Integration Testing is a strategy to test the *collaboration* of at least *two* *components.*

The nature of components regarded as units are the same as with Unit Testing. However, they can range from the class up to whole components in the system. Hence:

 Integration Testing

Integration Testing is a strategy to test the *collaboration* of at least *two* *classes.*

Given this definition, nearly every test which is not a unit test is an integration test. However, integration tests differ in their SUT scope: testing a SUT of two classes is far from testing a SUT made of the entire system.

1.3.1 Related concepts

With Integration Testing comes a number of related concepts, that stand outside the Unit Testing realm.

1.3.1.1 Required and provided interfaces

In fact, the previous diagram does not completely reflect the reality. Components do not depend on each other, but rather on a component method signature. In UML parlance, the term is coined *interface*.

 This is the same word as for the Java construct, but has a different meaning - context is everything!

A **required interface** is an interface a component depends on, while a **provided interface** is an interface offered by a component.

Our previous SUT can therefore be displayed as the following diagram stripped of its internal structure for better visibility.

b and e are interfaces. From A and D point of view, they are required interfaces, while from B and E point of view, they are provided interfaces.

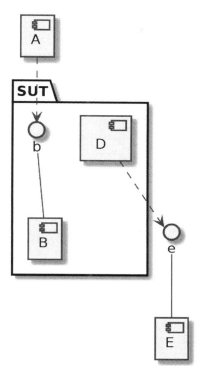

Fig. 1.5 - "Real" System Under Test modeling

1.3.1.2 Black and white-box testing

Once the SUT is defined, there are two strategies available to test it:

Black-box testing

In black-box testing, the SUT itself is considered the component to be tested **regardless of how it is structured**. This way, there is no need to worry about its internal workings. Calling the SUT with known parameters, and checking the output is enough.

 Black-box testing promotes higher independence between developers and testers as testers do not need to know about the structure of the SUT. Thus, if developers need to change it, there is no need to inform testers.

White-box testing

> In white-box testing, not only is the SUT output tested but also **its internal state** so knowing about the SUT's inner architecture becomes mandatory. This strategy lets us cover how the SUT is producing the expected result unlike the previous one: it is more precise, but also much more brittle since the internal design is more subject to change than provided interfaces, which belong to the public API.

1.3.2 Drawbacks of integration tests

Integration tests are different than unit tests in that they check collaboration between components. In this regard, they may suffer from drawbacks inherent to this specific nature. It is not that integration tests will for sure exhibit all of the following traits, but it will be likely to happen more often than not.

1.3.2.1 Brittle

The SUT probably has some outside dependencies. These may consist of one or more of the following:

- Databases
- Application servers
- Email (SMTP, POP, IMAP) servers
- File systems (*e.g.* for logging or for storage)
- FTP servers
- JMS queues
- In this day and age, web services, whether exposed through REST or SOAP

These are only a few examples, I'm sure most readers have experience with many others. If during execution of an integration test, the tested SUT relies on any dependency, chances are at one time or another it will fail, not because of the code but because the dependency is unavailable. With enough time, it is practically a certainty.

Hence, the alarm will be sounded for bad reasons - a false positive. Brittleness is a very bad property: if it occurs too frequently, people will get used to this test failing.

At this point, the test does not play its sentinel role anymore and you can put it in the trash bin. At one point or another, the test will fail because of a bug, not for the dependency being down but the team will not investigate because it will assume it is for the usual reason.

> Flaky tests are worse than having no tests, because a flaky test pollutes your build health and decreases the credibility of your suite.

Source: http://googletesting.blogspot.com/2013/08/how-google-team-tests-mobile-apps.html

Techniques on how to decrease brittleness will be detailed in *Chapter 3 - Test-Friendly Design*.

1.3.2.2 Slow

Though integration tests are not slow *per se*, they are slower than unit tests as a general rule:

- Most of the aforementioned dependencies performances are not on a par with standard in-memory code execution. With more than one dependency mandatory, it slows down integration tests even more.
- Besides, some integration tests may be asynchronous in nature. This requires polling until an assertion passes.

1.3.2.3 Hard to diagnose

In our craft, some developers advocate for Integration Testing **instead** of Unit Testing (and not as well as). This may be a problem when a test fails: in this case, it will be very hard to locate the root cause of the problem.

Fig. 1.6 - Multiple class collaboration

In the diagram above, picture the SUT containing all classes. Now, if a test fails, the defect could be located in many places: A, B, C, D, E but also in the interaction between A and B, B and C, C and D and D and E. Locating the defect will probably take some time to someone unfamiliar with the code.

With unit tests available, we could ensure the individual A, B, C, D and E classes run correctly (or not); if the integration test fails while all unit tests are successful, this means the defect is located in the collaboration between those classes.

1.3.3 Unit Testing vs Integration Testing?

With all these drawbacks, it is strange that one would want to use integration tests at all. However, they are the only way to test that software meets high-level expectations. As in everything related to software (some would even say in general), Return Over Investment (ROI) is the keyword. The higher the number of integration tests, the lower the ROI. Therefore, it is advisable to keep those tests for nominal scenarios - also known as happy paths, and not cover corner-cases; the latter is where Unit Testing really shines. In this way, the highest ROI can be achieved while keeping integration tests relevant.

Most of the time, Integration Testing is either crudely defined, wrongly understood or imperfectly used. In order to maximize the ROI, the most important guideline should be **the larger the SUT, the less the number of tests**:

- On one hand, when the SUT is the entire application, one should only test the most critical and common use-cases
- On the other hand, when the SUT is a single class as in the case of Unit Testing, one should provide the highest code coverage

The test organization should adopt a pyramidal structure, with many unit tests at the pyramid base and and less but broader integration tests at the top. The higher the number of classes collaborating, the lesser the number of tests.

 ## SUT scope trade-off

The smaller the SUT scope, the lower the confidence in the entire system. On the other hand, the larger the SUT scope, the more brittle, slower to run and harder to diagnose the integration tests will be.

1.4 Other testing flavors

Mutation Testing

Unit Testing is a harness for production code. However, nothing is done about the testing code itself. Mutation Testing tries to foster confidence in tests by changing the source code. "Good" tests will automatically detect the faulty behavior and fail, while tests still succeeding point to something fishy.

Changed source code is called a mutation, with a failing test killing the mutation and a successful one allowing it to survive.

Functional Testing

While Unit Testing asserts fine-grained behavior, Integration Testing does the same for coarse-grained behavior. Functional Testing is the ultimate form of Integration Testing where the tested behavior is the highest possible level, human-to-machine interaction (or machine-to-machine).

By using Functional Testing, user requirements such as "When the user clicks on this button, the list of all available cars are displayed" can be tested.

Security Testing

Security Testing is all about shipping a product that covers 6 basic security related notions: confidentiality, integrity, authentication, authorization, availability and non-repudiation. Note that some might not be required for each piece of software. Security Testing is orthogonal to Integration Testing. Readers interested in going further should invest time in browsing the Open Web Application Security Project (https://www.owasp.org).

Performance Testing

Performance Testing is a kind of testing performed on the integrated system as a whole on production-like infrastructure to assert performances are on a par with what is expected. Inside performance testing are subcategories:

- Load testing: loads the system under peak expected load. This is used to check the system has acceptable response time under "normal" load. This is by far the most common kind of performance testing.
- Stress testing: loads the system more and more until it breaks. This is used to check the system's upper load limit.

- Endurance testing: loads the system at fixed thresholds repeatedly over a long period of time. This is used to detect problems that cannot be detected over too short a period of time, such as memory leaks.

Performance testing does not belong to the scope of Integration Testing.

1.5 Summary

At this point, understanding of testing in general and Integration Testing in particular should be high. As seen previously, Unit Testing has some inherent limitations that need to be addressed in order to provide the best software possible. Integration Testing addresses the limitations of Unit Testing, at a cost. In the next chapter, simple testing tools used throughout the rest of the book will be described in detail.

2. Developer testing tools

In this chapter, we will have a look at two common frameworks that can help us develop maintainable tests.

The tools described here require software engineer proficiency, and the ability to code, compile and run Java code. They generally end up in the hands of developers, hence the section name.

 Though those frameworks were designed for unit-testing in mind, they can also be - **and are** - used for integration testing. Both are completely uncorrelated, so be somewhat wary with people telling you they are unit-testing their code base because they use JUnit - they do exist!

2.1 A time before our time

Before unit testing tools were available, developers wanting to unit-test their code had to rely upon a cheap and dirty trick. They used the class main() method to do such testing. This is what such a test looked like:

Code 2.1 - Using main() to test

```
1   public class Die implements Rollable {
2
3       private SecureRandom random = new SecureRandom();
4
5       public int roll() {
6           return random.nextInt(6) + 1;
7       }
8
9       public static void main(String... args) throws Exception {
10          Die die = new Die();
```

```
11        int roll = die.roll();
12        if (roll < 1 || roll > 6) {
13            throw new Exception("Bad die roll result : " + roll);
14        }
15    }
16 }
```

This approach was good enough in that it let us create a test application that scanned our class files, get their main() method by introspection (if any) and call it to check for test failures. However, it also had several drawbacks:

- It coupled real functional code and testing code in the same class, thus forcing testing behavior into production
- It made the main() method responsible for testing features. It did not account for classes providing a "functional" main() method for the application to run, *e.g.* classes that were entry points into the application such as with Swing applications
- Since there was no specialized Exception type thrown by failing test cases, we could not differentiate between a component in error or a test failure
- All test cases were put in the same method, mixing all test cases together. In the case of a failure, it was hard to readily assess which test failed
- All test code blurred into the same block, not distinguishing between initialization code, clean up code and testing code proper

2.2 Life-cycle phases

Unit testing frameworks provide a solution to the big ball of mud problem presented earlier. In particular, they follow a predefined life-cycle:

1. Initialization
2. Test case executions
3. Clean up

In Java code, this translates as follows:

Code 2.2 - Simple test structure

```
1   public class MyTestClass {
2
3       public void setUp() {
4           // Initialization code goes there
5       }
6
7       public void do_something() {
8           // Testing code goes there
9       }
10
11      public void tearDown() {
12          // Clean up code goes there
13      }
14  }
```

Calling setUp(), do_something() and tearDown() in this order will achieve the desired result.

Initialization or *set up*

The initialization phase prepares the context for upcoming test executions. It should at least create the instance to be tested. More complex tests may require advanced preparation, such as - but not limited to:

- Connecting to databases
- Populating databases with sample data
- Starting application servers
- Deploying applications to the application servers
- Connecting to JMS queues

> When a connection or a similar object is opened during initialization, it must be kept as a reference so as to be closed later in the clean up phase.

Case executions

The execution phase refers to the test proper. Once set-up has run its course, all test cases are executed. As a general rule, a test case must contain one or more assertions. A case not containing any assertion should be treated with suspicion. Checking an exception is thrown is considered an assertion.

Clean up or *tear down*

The tear down phase is intended to clean up what happened during the previous phases. It must at least be symmetric in regard to initialization *e.g.* releasing a database connection obtained previously; yet, it may also clean up test cases side-effects: removing database data, log files, etc.

⚷ When to setup instances?

- Declare the class to be tested as an attribute of the test class
- Initialize the attrbute instance in the setup method body
- Initialize required dependencies either in the setup method body if they are valid across all test methods or in each test method if they are only for this particular method

```java
public class MyTestCase {

    private MyClassUnderTest underTest;

    public void setUp() {
        underTest = new MyClassUnderTest();
    }

    public void should_do_that() {
        MyClassDependency dep = new MyClassDependency();
        underTest.doThat(dep);
    }
}
```

2.3 JUnit

JUnit (http://junit.org/) is the first and most popular unit testing framework for Java. It was created by Kent Beck and Erich Gamma. It brought many ideas that are now widespread in other unit testing tools, including the colored bar to display success or failure as popularized by the motto:

"Keep the bar green to keep the code clean!"

It was so successful, that many languages have a native port (PHPUnit, CppUnit, etc.). It is now even common to speak of xUnit framework in reference to them.

2.3.1 Basics

In order for a method to be referenced as a test case, it should be annotated with `@org.junit.Test`.

 @Test annotations can be set at the class **and** the method level. The former should be discouraged (and the latter enforced), for it implicitly makes **every method** of the annotated class a test case to be run.

JUnit life-cycle phases are limited to:

- `@org.junit.Before` and `@org.junit.After` each `@org.junit.Test` execution
- `@org.junit.BeforeClass` and `@org.junit.AfterClass` execution of all tests of a specific class. In this case, initialization/clean-up code will run once regardless of the number of executed tests. Annotated methods are required to be `static`.

Assertions are grouped in static methods of the `org.junit.Assert` patterned as `assertSomething()`. Such methods include:

- `Assert.assertTrue(boolean)`

- Assert.assertFalse(boolean)
- Assert.assertEquals(T expected, T actual)
- Assert.assertNotEquals(T expected, T actual)
- Assert.assertArrayEquals(T[] expected, T[] actual)
- Assert.assertArrayNotEquals(T[] expected, T[] actual)
- etc.

 All methods accept an additional String argument that can optionally be used as the failure message. Most of the time, using this additional parameter just adds confusion: use it with care.

As code says a thousand words, let us use our newfound knowledge to test the previous Die example with the JUnit framework.

Code 2.3 - Simple JUnit test for the Die class

```
import static org.junit.Assert.assertTrue;

import org.junit.Before;
import org.junit.Test;
import org.junit.runners.JUnit4;
import org.junit.runner.RunWith;

@RunWith(JUnit4.class)
public class JunitDieTest {

    private Die die;

    @Before
    public void setUp() {
        die = new Die();
    }

    @Test
    public void roll_should_be_between_1_included_and_6_included() {
        int roll = die.roll();
```

```
21        assertTrue(roll >= 1);
22        assertTrue(roll <= 6);
23    }
24 }
```

The single assert rule

Each test method should only provide:

- A single assert, being the *raison d'etre* of the test method
- Or a tightly bound group of asserts, for example:

```
Assert.assertNotNull(list);
Assert.assertFalse(list.isEmpty());
Assert.assertEquals(1, list.size());
```

This way, each assert is a little more restrictive than the previous and if the test fails, we will know **exactly** the reason (the list was null, it was empty or it had more than a single element).

Notice the annotation on the class itself: a JUnit runner is responsible for effectively executing methods annotated with @Test. JUnit provides a org.junit.runners.JUnit4 runner to be used as default, but other runners can be used for specific use-cases.

In order to specify a runner, annotate the test class with @ org.junit.runner.RunWith and set the runner class as its value. Further runner setup depends on the runner's nature.

Finally, check both assert at the end of the roll_should_be_between_1_included_-and_6_included() method: when *either* one fails, it will throw a core Java java.lang.AssertionError, thus interrupting method execution and directing the control flow up the method stack, as in standard Java code.

This means after the first failed assertion, no code in the method will be executed.

> However, other test methods will.

2.3.2 Expected exceptions

As seen above, failed assertions will result in failures. However, failures may also be explicitly invoked:

```
Assert.failure("Failure message");
```

 The failure() method is also available with no argument though it is highly discouraged to use it. Nothing is more frustrating than having a test fail, looking at the log and having no clues about failure reasons.

Return values are not the only possible results from a method execution; in particular, exceptions may also be thrown. In this case, unexpected exceptions will be categorized as errors, while expected ones will be categorized as failures.

In this case, a possible naive implementation to test for an exception is the following:

Code 2.4 - Testing for expected exception

```
1   public class CarFactoryService {
2
3       public Car assemble(CarPart... part) throw AssemblyException {
4           // Assemble car from car parts
5           return new Car();
6       }
7   }
8
9   import static org.junit.Assert.fail;
10
11  import org.junit.Before;
12  import org.junit.Test;
```

```
13   import org.junit.runners.JUnit4;
14   import org.junit.runner.RunWith;
15
16   @RunWith(JUnit4.class)
17   public class NaiveCarFactoryServiceTest {
18
19       private CarFactoryService carFactoryService;
20
21       @Before
22       public void setUp() {
23           carFactoryService = new CarFactoryService();
24       }
25
26       @Test
27       public void should_throw_exception_when_one_part_unavailable() {
28           // Parts come from somewhere
29           CarPart part = ...;
30           try {
31               carFactoryService.assemble(part);
32               fail("Expected exception AssemblyException not thrown");
33           } catch (AssemblyException e) {
34               // Expected exception
35           }
36       }
37   }
```

Yet, this code is verbose and is a candidate for some syntactic conciseness. Fortunately, this is available with the expected attribute of the @Test annotation. The previous snippet can therefore be replaced with the following:

Code 2.5 - Better testing for expected exception

```
1   import org.junit.Before;
2   import org.junit.Test;
3   import org.junit.runners.JUnit4;
4   import org.junit.runner.RunWith;
5
6   @RunWith(JUnit4.class)
7   public class JunitCarFactoryServiceTest {
8
9       private CarFactoryService carFactoryService;
10
11      @Before
12      public void setUp() {
13          carFactoryService = new CarFactoryService();
14      }
15
16      @Test(expected = AssemblyException.class)
17      public void should_throw_exception_when_one_part_unavailable()
18          throws Exception {
19          // Part come from somewhere
20          CarPart part = ...;
21          carFactoryService.assemble(part);
22      }
23  }
```

2.3.3 Launching JUnit

There are several ways to launch JUnit to run test-cases:

- Through the command-line

```
java -cp /path/to/junit.jar org.junit.runner.JUnitCore <TestClass>
```

- Through common build tools, such as Ant or Maven
- Through your favorite IDE. Eclipse, NetBeans and IntelliJ IDEA all integrate with JUnit very well

2.3.4 Grouping tests

As an example, the `org.junit.runners.Suite` runner class is able to group other JUnit test classes, so that running the suite will run all referenced test classes. The associated `@org.junit.runners.Suite` is mandatory to detail which test classes should be run.

Code 2.6 - JUnit suite example

```
1  import org.junit.runner.RunWith;
2  import org.junit.runners.Suite;
3
4  @RunWith(Suite.class)
5  @Suite.SuiteClasses({ TestClass1.class, TestClass2.class, TestClass3.class })
6  public class TestSuite {}
```

2.3.5 Lifecycle hooks

JUnit offers two lifecycle hooks:

- As seen in example 2.3 above, one hook is called before running each test, with the help of the `@org.junit.Before` annotation. Methods annotated as such are required to be `public`
- The other one is called before the class's **first** test method is executed; methods have to be annotated with `@org.junit.BeforeClass` and are required to be `static` (as well as `public`)

Of course, corresponding annotations are available for methods to be executed after tests in the form of `@org.junit.After` and `@org.junit.AfterClass`.

 Different tools provide different life-cycle hooks; clean-up can be configured to take place before each test case, before the whole suite or before a framework-specific hook, as well as after each hook. Be aware of those hooks so so that you execute the desired code at the right time.

2.3.6 Ordering tests

Unit Testing frowns on the ordering of tests, for test cases should not rely on each other or on state. However, what goes for Unit Testing should not always blindly be applied to Integration Testing. In particular, having multiple ordered fine-grained methods with each method asserting the state of the system may be required for white-box testing.

JUnit provides some basic features regarding ordering. One can choose to order by annotating the test class with @org.junit.FixMethodOrder and use one of the three following values:

1. org.junit.runners.JVM for no ordering at all
2. org.junit.runners.DEFAULT for **deterministic but not predictable** ordering
3. org.junit.runners.NAME_ASCENDING for ordering based on method name

Code 2.7 - JUnit ordering example

```
1   import org.junit.FixMethodOrder;
2   import org.junit.Test;
3   import org.junit.runner.RunWith;
4   import org.junit.runners.JUnit4;
5   import org.junit.runners.MethodSorters;
6
7   @RunWith(JUnit4.class)
8   @FixMethodOrder(MethodSorters.NAME_ASCENDING)
9   public class OrderedTestClass {
10
11      @Test public void firstTest() {}
12      @Test public void secondTest() {}
13      @Test public void thirdTest() {}
14      @Test public void fourthTest() {}
15  }
```

Using method names as the sort criteria enforces some artificial naming - or is a source of potential mistakes. In the previous snippet, methods run in the following order: firstMethod(), fourthMethod(), secondMethod() and thirdMethod(). It is not the most intuitive sorting possible.

2.4 TestNG

The TestNG (http://testng.org) framework - for *Test New Generation,* was started by Eric Beust in order to address JUnit 3 limitation, specifically regarding relying on pattern matching (*i.e.* it was mandatory for test class names to end with `Test` and test method names to start with `test`) to find test methods. TestNG offered Java 5 annotations that were just introduced at that time as a replacement, while still using the JUnit 3 engine underneath.

With time, differences between JUnit and TestNG have somewhat blurred, though the edge is still on TestNG's side. For Integration Testing, the following features are still very much relevant:

- Sophisticated launch configuration
- Richer life-cycle hook options for initialization and clean-up
- Improved ordering capabilities

TestNG's test annotation is `@org.testng.annotations.Test`.

2.4.1 Basics and checked exceptions

As with JUnit, TestNG also offers an assertion class `org.testng.Assert` with the same methods as `org.junit.Assert`:

- `Assert.assertTrue(boolean)`
- `Assert.assertFalse(boolean)`
- `Assert.assertEquals(T actual, T expected)`
- `Assert.assertNotEquals(T actual, T expected)`
- `Assert.assertArrayEquals(T[] actual, T[] expected)`
- `Assert.assertArrayNotEquals(T[] actual, T[] expected)`
- etc.

A huge source of confusion is that TestNG first parameter is *actual* and the second *expected* which is the opposite of JUnit. You have been warned!

Assert also has a static `fail()` method.

Finally, expected exceptions are naturally configured with the `expectedExceptions` attribute of the `@Test` annotation.

The following snippet is a port of the previous JUnit code to TestNG:

Code 2.8 - Simple TestNG test for the Die class

```
1   import static org.testng.Assert.assertTrue;
2
3   import org.testng.annotations.BeforeMethod;
4   import org.testng.annotations.Test;
5
6   public class TestngDieTest {
7
8       private Die die;
9
10      @BeforeMethod public void setUp() {
11          die = new Die();
12      }
13
14      @Test
15      public void roll_should_be_between_1_and_6_included() {
16          int roll = die.roll();
17          assertTrue(roll >= 1);
18          assertTrue(roll <= 6);
19      }
20  }
```

2.4.2 Launching TestNG

TestNG can be launched through the same options as for JUnit:

- Through the command-line, by explicitly referencing which test cases to run

```
java -cp path/to/testng.jar org.testng.TestNG \
    -groups <Group1>,<Group2> \
    -testclass <TestClass1>,<TestClass2> \
```

- The -cp java parameter defines the classpath. The testng.jar is of course required.
- The -groups parameter tells TestNG which groups to run.
- The -testclass parameter tells TestNG which individual test class to run.

• Through the command-line, by referencing one or more configuration files

```
java -cp path/to/testng.jar org.testng.TestNG conf1.xml, conf2.xml
```

Referenced XMLs are TestNG configuration files in the TestNG proprietary format (http://testng.org/doc/documentation-main.html#testng-xml).

• Through the same standard build tools and common IDEs as JUnit.

 TestNG plugins TestNG plugins are not as widespread as JUnit but they are available for all major IDEs:
- Eclipse (http://testng.org/doc/eclipse.html)
- IntelliJ IDEA (http://testng.org/doc/idea.html)
- and NetBeans (http://wiki.netbeans.org/TestNG)))

2.4.3 Grouping tests

While JUnit is limited to grouping using test suites, TestNG offers many more ways to group test cases.

A TestNG group is strangely similar to a JUnit suite. Putting a test method in a group is as easy as setting the groups attribute on the @org.testng.annotations.Test annotation.

Code 2.9 - TestNG grouping example

```
1   import org.testng.annotations.Test;
2
3   public class GroupExampleTest {
4
5       @Test(groups = "mygroup")
6       public void sampleTestMethod() {
7           // Test something here
8       }
9   }
```

Note that test methods can belong to as many groups as necessary, allowing for powerful grouping strategies. For example, we could define both architecture-layer-related groups as well as use-case-related groups. This way, and depending on the context, we could have a dedicated continuous integration job for each.

Code 2.10 - Cross group example

```
1   import org.testng.annotations.Test;
2
3   public class CrossGroupExampleTest {
4
5       @Test(groups = {"servicelayer", "use_case1"})
6       public void use_case_1_in_service_layer() { ... }
7
8       @Test(groups = {"daolayer", "use_case1"})
9       public void use_case_1_in_dao_layer() { ... }
10
11      @Test(groups = {"servicelayer", "use_case2"})
12      public void use_case_2_in_service_layer() { ... }
13
14      @Test(groups = {"daolayer", "use_case2"})
15      public void use_case_2_in_dao_layer() { ... }
16  }
```

Alternatively, we could use the TestNG configuration file to achieve the same, decoupling grouping from the code's responsibilities.

What really sets TestNG above JUnit in this area is how its launcher can be configured to run a specific set of test cases, using group, package, class and method combinations.

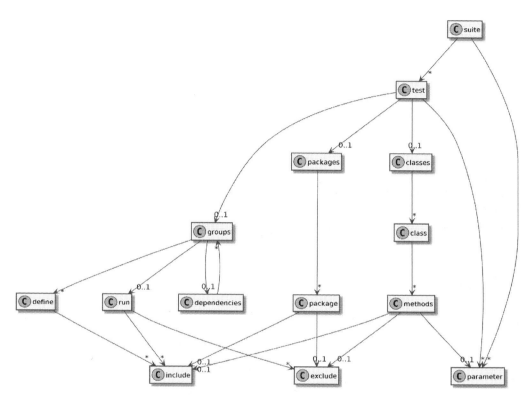

Fig. 2.1 - TestNG configuration model

Explicit reference

Explicit reference is just that: TestNG is told which groups, packages, classes and/or methods need to be executed. TestNG runs them and outputs their results.

Code 2.11 - TestNG explicit reference configuration file

```
1    <test name="DaoAndUseCaseOneInService">
2        <groups>
3            <run>
4                <include name="daolayer"/>
5            </run>
6        </groups>
7        <classes>
8            <class name="CrossGroupExampleTest">
9                <methods>
10                    <include name="use_case_1_in_service_layer" />
11                </methods>
12            </class>
13        </classes>
14    </test>
```

Given the previous CrossGroupExampleTest test class, the following configuration file would run the following:

- use_case_1_in_dao_layer() and use_case_2_in_dao_layer(), because
  they belong to the daolayer group
- use_case_1_in_service_layer(), for it it referenced by its fully-qualified
  class name and its method name

use_case_2_in_service_layer() will not be executed because it matches no
element in the configuration file.

Pattern matching

In addition to explicit reference, we may reference test cases to be executed
according to part of their names and use joker characters for the rest - as in
typical pattern matching.

Code 2.12 - TestNG pattern matching configuration file

```
1    <test name="AllMyMethodsAndIntegrationTestPackage">
2        <packages>
3            <package name="ch.frankel.integrationtest.*" />
4        </packages>
5        <classes>
6            <class name="CrossGroupExampleTest">
7                <methods>
8                    <include name="use_case_1_*" />
9                </methods>
10           </class>
11       </classes>
12   </test>
```

The previous configuration file will run the following test methods:

- All from the package ch.frankel.integrationtest
- use_case_1_in_dao_layer() and use_case_1_in_service_layer() as both their names match the configured pattern.

use_case_2_in_dao_layer() and use_case_2_in_service_layer() will not be executed because they are neither in a class from the ch.frankel.integrationtest package nor do their names match "use_case_1_*".

 In practice, use of this feature should be carefully considered as it makes test execution depend on method names. Not only does it tend to make method names artificial, those may also be subject to refactoring changes and thus completely be removed from (or added to) the test configuration as an unexpected side-effect.

Exclusion

Up to this point, we learned how to add tests to the list of to-be-executed tests. However, some use-cases may be more easily described by using "all apart from this and that" instead of "this and that and those". This is the goal of the <exclude> tag, which takes precedence over <include> tags, so be careful.

Code 2.13 - TestNG exclude configuration file

```
1   <test name="DaoSaveUseCase1">
2       <groups>
3           <run>
4               <include name="daolayer"/>
5               <exclude name="use_case_1"/>
6           </run>
7       </groups>
8   </test>
```

The previous configuration file will run all the test methods of the DAO layer, save those of Use-Case 1:

- use_case_1_in_service_layer() and use_case_2_in_service_layer() will not be executed because they do not belong to the daolayer group
- use_case_1_in_dao_layer() belongs to the daolayer group but will not be executed because it also belongs to the uc1 group
- use_case_2_in_dao_layer() will be executed because it belongs to the daolayer group but not the uc1 one

2.4.4 Lifecycle hooks

As compared to JUnit, TestNG offers many more lifecycle hooks, one for each TestNG group level:

- @org.testng.annotations.BeforeSuite, invoked once before any single test of the configured suite is executed
- @org.testng.annotations.BeforeTest, invoked once before any test class referenced inside the <test> tag configuration file is executed
- @org.testng.annotations.BeforeGroups, invoked once before any of the configured groups of tests is executed
- @org.testng.annotations.BeforeClass, invoked once before the class's **first** test method is executed, and similar to JUnit's @BeforeClass. However, it does not require the method to be static.

- `@org.testng.annotations.BeforeMethod`, invoked once before each test method is executed, and similar to JUnit's `@Before`

Symmetric `@AfterXXX` annotations are also available *e.g.* `@AfterMethod` and so on.

 Hooks will be called in the described order for initialization, and in the opposite order for cleanup.

2.4.5 Ordering

As with JUnit, TestNG offers test ordering capabilities, but they are more robust than JUnit in that they do not rely on method names.

`@Test` accepts two array attributes:

- `dependsOnMethods` lists all methods that must be executed before the current one
- `dependsOnGroups` lists all groups that must be executed before the method

The TestNG engine will parse all test methods and their dependencies and compute an acyclic resolution graph that provides a solution.

 It is the developer's responsibility to manage dependencies so as to provide at least one possible solution. If there are any cyclic dependencies (*i.e.* if no single acyclic graph can be computed), TestNG will throw a `org.testng.TestNGException` with the message "The following methods have cyclic dependencies".

For example, the following test classes ensure that the DAO layer test cases will run before the Service layer ones. The rest however (*e.g.* which dao will be executed first) is non-deterministic.

Code 2.14 - TestNG group ordering

```
1   import org.testng.annotations.Test;
2
3   public class TireDaoTest {
4
5       @Test(groups = "daolayer")
6       public void should_load_tire_by_pk() { ... }
7   }
8
9   public class EngineDaoTest {
10
11      @Test(groups = "daolayer")
12      public void should_load_engine_by_pk() { ... }
13  }
14
15  public class CarFactoryServiceTest {
16
17      @Test(groups = "servicelayer", dependsOnGroups  = "daolayer")
18      public void should_assemble_when_all_parts_available() { ... }
19
20      @Test(groups = "servicelayer", dependsOnGroups  = "daolayer")
21      public void should_throw_ex_when_1_part_unavailable() { ... }
22  }
```

 # Scenario with multiple steps rule

Compared to JUnit, TestNG ordering provides for a deterministic and **relevant** ordering. This is important for Integration Testing as it allows for small test methods, each being a step in the overall scenario. This way, a failing scenario will be self-describing as to the reason why if test methods have been named in a relevant way.

For example, imagine a batch process to be tested that connects to a database, pulls data from it, creates a file with that data and puts the file in a specific folder. With a single test method, a detailed look is necessary. By mapping each step to a dedicated method (unless more details are required and steps have to be further broken down), a quick glance will reveal the method name and thus the step with the error should the scenario fail.

2.5 Summary

In this chapter, two similar testing tools were looked at, JUnit and TestNG, that may be used to create executable tests by providing some required capabilities:

- Launching tests (of course)
- Asserting some predefined condition(s)
- Initializing and cleaning execution context
- Grouping tests that may need to be launched together, based on a relevant criterion, *e.g.* layer or use-case
- Ordering tests in a test suite

Both of them can be used in Unit Testing and Integration Testing: they are just that, tools, and we use them as we see fit. However, TestNG is more convenient to use for Integration Testing, as it allows for more options regarding initialization/cleanup, grouping and ordering.

Whichever tool is used, one should be consistent with it. The first rule is to decide on a single framework for a project (or even the whole enterprise), as some of their features are configured in different ways (the inverted parameter order in `Assert` is really nasty). Barring that, one could segregate them by rules, *e.g.* using JUnit for Unit Testing and TestNG for Integration Testing.

However, choosing and using a test framework is by no way enough to do proper Integration Testing. The next chapter will describe how to design a system to allow for only parts of the system to be tested.

3. Test-Friendly Design

In the previous chapters, we have described functional testing, along with its pros and cons. Some of the latter comes from having to consider the entire application as the System Under Test. In order to improve our tests execution speed and focus on the parts of the application deemed important, the SUT can be reduced using some techniques.

This chapter covers:

- Dependency Injection, a very common technique to achieve decoupling between classes
- How to enable it in application design
- Some definitions of set dependencies, depending on the role they play during test execution
- Testing frameworks that can help us leverage this technique in tests
- And finally, a couple of tools to help us even further

3.1 Reducing coupling

In the Object-Oriented Programming world, designing applications has been taught as a collection of classes collaborating, each class having a single responsibility (http://en.wikipedia.org/wiki/Single_responsibility_principle).

This sometimes tangled mess of dependent classes makes it initially hard to isolate a part of the system as a SUT, if only because classes need to create new dependency objects for them to use.

```
1   public class Caller {
2
3       public Concrete doSomething() {
4           Concrete c = new Concrete();
5           // Do something with c
6           return c;
7       }
8   }
```

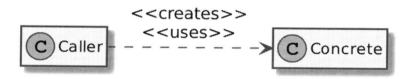

Fig. 3.1 - Strongest coupling possible

Nonetheless, there are a couple of techniques to decrease coupling.

3.1.1 Decoupling techniques

Programming to interfaces

Programming to interfaces means our method signatures should use the highest possible abstraction in the class hierarchy. This way, coupling to implementation-specific details is kept at a minimum; in turn, this makes for more reusable code.

```
1   public class Caller {
2
3       public Abstraction doSomething() {
4           Concrete c = new Concrete();
5           // Do something with c
6           return c;
7       }
8   }
```

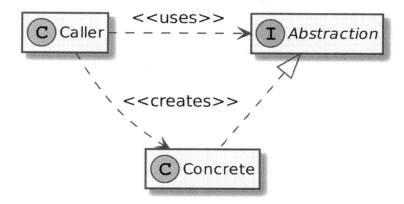

Fig. 3.2 - Programming to interfaces

Factory Method

Factory Method (http://en.wikipedia.org/wiki/Factory_pattern) is a Design Pattern described by the Gang of Four in the famous book *Design Patterns - Elements of Reusable Object-Oriented Software.*

Factory is a *creational* pattern, and its responsibility is to create new objects while isolating the caller class from the exact returned type. In essence, the caller asks the Factory for an instance and the Factory provides it. The returned instance may depend on parameters, on the context, or anything.

For example, the Factory could return "dummy" objects in a testing context, and "real" objects in a production environment.

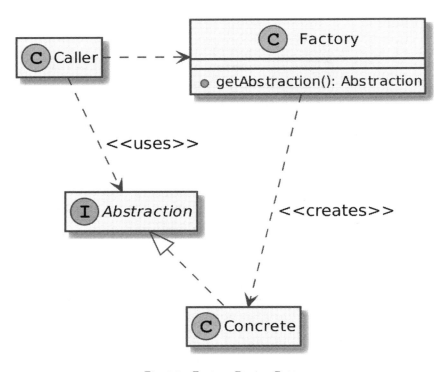

Fig. 3.3 - Factory Design Pattern

Service Locator

Service Locator (http://en.wikipedia.org/wiki/Service_locator_pattern) is a Design Pattern meant to wrap the way of retrieving objects from a registry under an abstraction layer. Its class diagram closely resembles the above Factory, but Service Locator's concern is to provide the required instances, not create them.

Dependency Injection

Factory and Service Locator both require the class needingthe objects to **actively** query them to return the dependency, hence the term Caller in the diagram above. With Dependency Injection (or DI), the class becomes passive as it has nothing to do at runtime: it is the responsibility of the DI module to provide the required dependency.

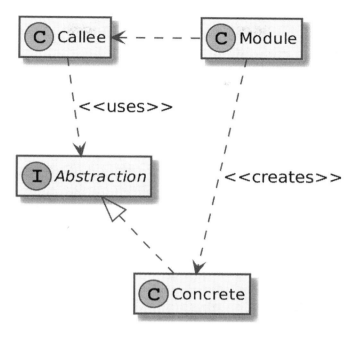

Fig. 3.4 - Dependency Injection

In the above diagram, the arrow direction has been reversed: our new `Callee` is now completely independent of any Factory, Service Locator or even DI Module!

3.1.2 Enabling Dependency Injection

Dependency Injection can be enabled in three different ways, the last option depending on the exact implementation:

1. Setter injection requires the callee to provide a setter for each required dependency:

```
1    public class Callee {
2
3        private Abstraction abstraction;
4
5        public void setAbstraction(Abstraction abstraction) {
6            this.abstraction = abstraction;
7        }
8    }
```

2. Constructor injection requires the callee to provide a constructor accepting the dependency as a parameter:

```
1    public class Callee {
2
3        private Abstraction abstraction;
4
5        public Callee(Abstraction abstraction) {
6            this.abstraction = abstraction;
7        }
8    }
```

Constructor injection favors immutability, and should be preferred over setter injection, since required dependencies should not generally change during the life-cycle of the callee.

3. Finally, field injection only requires the callee to have a corresponding field.

```
1    public class Callee {
2        private Abstraction abstraction;
3    }
```

 # Field injection pitfall

Field injection relies on some reflection magic from the DI framework. In order to test code that is using field injection, the testing framework also requires the same magic: before putting such a requirement on the tools, one should really consider the added value of going this way (which does not actually exist).

3.1.3 Putting the pieces together

It is time to take a real-world example of an applied design: let us design an e-commerce platform. One of the features of this platform is to let customers order products. This could translate into the following classes:

- A CustomerRepository to get the customer from the database
- A ProductRepository to get ordered products from the database
- An OrderRepository to store new orders
- An OrderService that "executes" the order. Internally, its creates the order, associates it with both customer and products and finally passes it to the repository for persistent storage.

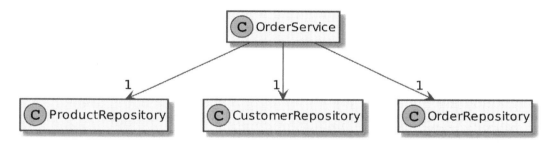

Fig. 3.5 - Service dependent on multiple repositories

It seems the OrderService is quite dependent on other classes and would make a nice candidate for dependency injection. Using our newfound knowledge, let us design it so it is ready for DI.

Code 3.1 - Injection-ready class

```
1   public class OrderService {
2
3       private OrderRepository orderRepository;
4       private CustomerRepository customerRepository;
5       private ProductRepository productRepository;
6
7       public OrderService(CustomerRepository customerRepository,
8                           OrderRepository orderRepository,
9                           ProductRepository productRepository) {
10
11          this.customerRepository = customerRepository;
12          this.orderRepository = orderRepository;
13          this.productRepository = productRepository;
14      }
15  }
```

This is easy enough. Now it is time to leverage DI to test `OrderService`.

3.2 Double definitions

With our DI-friendly design, setting a dependency in a test is quite easy. Setting the right one however may be quite complex. Some years ago, crafting our own implementation was the only way to go. This created a whole new bunch of (possibly bug-ridden) code. Before using a library, however, we need to define the goals to be achieved:

Dummy

Dummies play no role during test executions. When using constructor injection, passing `null` is enough whereas with setter injection, nothing is required.

Code 3.2 - Dummy example

```
1    import org.testng.annotations.BeforeMethod;
2
3    public class OrderServiceTest {
4
5        private OrderService serviceUnderTest;
6
7        @BeforeMethod
8        protected void setUp() {
9            serviceUnderTest =
10               new OrderService(new CustomerRepository(), null, null);
11       }
12
13       // Tests follow
14   }
```

Fake

Fakes are working implementations. However, they are not suitable for use in production, for one reason or another. For example, an in-memory data-source may be used for testing for ease of use and performance reasons but it is not persistent and cannot be be used in a real environment.

Stub Stubs are used for verifying purposes, either the state they are in or that some method has been called on them after test execution(s). In the following snippet, a stub to assert that the repository has performed saving is created:

Code 3.3 - Class to test and associated test

```
1    import java.util.*;
2
3    public class CachingOrderRepository extends OrderRepository {
4
5        private List<Order> cachedOrders = new ArrayList<>();
6
7        public Order save(Order order) {
8            Order savedOrder = super.save(order);
9            cachedOrders.add(order);
```

```
10              return savedOrder;
11          }
12
13      public List<Order> getCachedOrders() {
14              return cachedOrders;
15          }
16  }
17
18  import org.testng.annotations.*;
19
20  import java.util.List;
21
22  import static org.testng.Assert.assertEquals;
23  import static org.testng.Assert.assertFalse;
24
25  public class CachingOrderRepositoryTest {
26
27      private OrderService serviceUnderTest;
28      private CachingOrderRepository orderRepository =
29                                      new CachingOrderRepository();
30
31      @BeforeMethod
32      protected void setUp() {
33
34          serviceUnderTest = new OrderService(
35              new CustomerRepository(),
36              orderRepository,
37              new ProductRepository());
38      }
39
40      @Test
41      public void placing_an_order_should_return_the_new_order() {
42
43          Customer customer;
44          Product product;
45
46          // Somehow get customer and product
47
```

```
48          Order order = serviceUnderTest.order(
49                          customer.getId(), product.getId());
50
51          List<Order> placedOrders = orderRepository.getCachedOrders();
52
53          assertFalse(placedOrders.isEmpty());
54          assertEquals(placedOrders.size(), 1);
55          assertEquals(placedOrders.get(0), order);
56      }
57  }
```

In the example above, the `CachingOrderRepository` instance plays the role of the stub.

Mock

Mocks are specific doubles programmed with some expected behavior, regarding the test being executed. As opposed to stubs, this behavior is not meant to assert but to provide data. In the following snippet, a mock to provide a hardcoded customer is shown:

```
1   public class HarcodedCustomerRepository extends CustomerRepository {
2
3       public Customer load(Long pk) {
4           Customer customer = new Customer();
5           // Set customer data
6           return customer;
7       }
8   }
```

This way, when the `OrderRepository` is set the `HarcodedCustomerRepository` during the test, the latter will load the desired customer during the order-placing process.

Test doubles may be necessary, but the previous code snippets showed us they were not costless. Stubs and mocks are code, and should be tested as such... If we reason about testing cost, it is clear those test doubles are not free.

Yet, it is not necessary to reinvent the wheel, as some smart people have already thought about that, and provide us with useful frameworks:

- Mockito is dedicated to creating mocks and stubs. Alternative frameworks include EasyMock (http://easymock.org/) and JMock (http://jmock.org/).
- Spring Test, although being part of the Spring framework, has some ready-to-use Fakes and can be used with no dependency on the rest of the libraries.
- Mockrunner also provides out-of-the-box Fakes

 Spring Test does not provide Fake objects aimed at the Java Messaging Service API (JMS); use MockRunner for that.

3.3 Mockito

Mockito (http://mockito.org/) is a powerful framework which aims to create objects that serve as both mocks and stubs without hassle.

The heart of Mockito is the static BDDMockito.mock(Class<T>) method; it can be used either with a class or interface parameter:

```
List<Person> persons = BDDMockito.mock(List.class);
LinkedList<Person> persons2 = BDDMockito.mock(LinkedList.class);
```

Mocking and generics

Note the code above creates lists of unknown types but they are assigned to lists of Person: this will create unchecked assignments warnings at compile time. Removing this warning requires adding `@SuppressWarnings("unchecked")` on the assignment.

3.3.1 Stubbing

Once an object has been created with Mockito, it is simple to stub it using the static `Mockito.mock(Class<T>)` method.

The Stubbing API looks like the following (do not be afraid, though, it is easy to use).

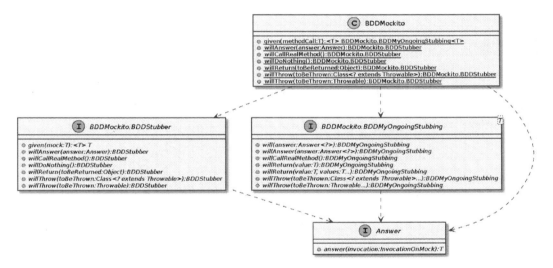

Fig. 3.6 - Mockito stubbing API

There are a couple of use-cases this lets us address.

 All the following snippets assume `import static org.mockito.BDDMockito.*`.

3.3.1.1 Exception-throwing stubs

In order to test unexpected cases, exception-throwing needs to be simulated. The static BDDMockito.willThrow() method stubs such behavior:

Code 3.4 - Expression-throwing

```
CustomerRepository repository = mock(CustomerRepository.class);

Exception e = new IllegalArgumentException();
// Set data on the exception

given(repository.load(1L)).willThrow(e);
repository.load(1L); // Will throw e
```

 Note that if extra data is not needed on the Exception as is the case in the previous snippet, Mockito can create the instance for us.

Code 3.5 - Simpler expression-throwing

```
CustomerRepository repository = mock(CustomerRepository.class);

given(repository.load(1L)).willThrow(IllegalArgumentException.class);
repository.load(1L); // Will throw a default instance
```

This way does not work if the stubbed method does not return a value, *i.e* its signature is set as void. In this case, the syntax should be reversed instead:

Code 3.6 - Void exception-throwing

```
OrderRepository repository = mock(OrderRepository.class);

willThrow(IllegalArgumentException.class)
        .given(repository).save(any(Order.class));
repository.save(new Order());
```

This reversed syntax allows for passing either exception instances or an exception class, as the standard one.

3.3.1.2 Result-returning stubs

During test executions, methods returning a specific result might be required. Using Mockito, this can be achieved with the static BDDMockito.willReturn() method:

Code 3.7 - Result-returning

```
Customer customer = new Customer();
// Set customer data

CustomerRepository repository = mock(CustomerRepository.class);

given(repository.load(1L)).willReturn(customer);
assertSame(repository.load(1L), customer);
```

When called, if the parameter value is not one expected by Mockito (different from 1L in this case), it will simply return null.

3.3.1.3 Any parameter

Should more flexibility be needed, Mockito also offers the Matcher API. Matchers are a great way to tell Mockito to be more lenient regarding parameters, *e.g.* always return the same value when matching a parameter value. The Matchers class offers the following methods:

- anyXXX() where XXX is a primitive type (boolean, char, byte, short, int, long, float, double)
- anyY() where Y is a collection type belonging to either Collection, List, Set and Map
- anyYOf(Class<T>) where Y belongs to the same collection types as above, matching only properly genericized collections
- any(Class<T>) only matches instances of the argument class
- anyObject() (and its shorter form any()) matches any object, including null
- Finally, anyVarargs() matches any number of instances of any type

Therefore, to be completely argument-independent, our first code snippet can be rewritten like this:

Code 3.8 - Stubbing for any parameter

```
Customer customer = new Customer();
CustomerRepository repository = mock(CustomerRepository.class);

given(repository.load(any(Long.class))).willReturn(customer);

assertSame(repository.load(1L), customer);
assertSame(repository.load(2L), customer);
assertSame(repository.load(null), customer);
```

 ## Keep Matchers simple and stupid

Mockito has more matching features than those described: there are other methods in the Matchers class as well as the AdditionalMatchers class. However, they should be avoided since they make the test more complex, less readable and more costly to maintain.

3.3.1.4 Contextual stubs

If returning different results depending on the context - including parameter values - become necessary, additional stubbing method have to be coded:

```
given(repository.load(2L)).willReturn(customer2);
given(repository.load(3L)).willReturn(customer3);
```

This will lead to exponential maintainability costs when the number of different returned instances grows. In order to address that, Mockito provides the static BDDMockito.willAnswer() method. Whereas willReturn() is constrained to a single object, willAnswer() is able to vary the returned result through the use of the Answer interface (or with Java 8, a simple lambda):

Code 3.9 - Contextual stubbing

```
CustomerRepository repository = mock(CustomerRepository.class);

Customer customer1 = new Customer();
Customer customer2 = new Customer();

given(repository.load(anyLong())).willAnswer(a -> {

        Object[] args = a.getArguments();

        Long pk = (Long) args[0];

        if (pk == null) return null;
        if (pk == 1) return customer1;
        if (pk == 2) return customer2;
        return null;
});

// when then
assertSame(repository.load(1L), customer1);
assertSame(repository.load(2L), customer2);
assertSame(repository.load(null), null);
```

Complexity alert

Using this kind of contextual behavior is a sure sign of too much testing at once. Remember it is preferable to have a simple disjointed test setup in each test case than a single master initialization in the setup. A better design would be the following:

Code 3.10 - Decreasing test setup complexity

```
1  import org.testng.annotations.BeforeMethod;
2  import org.testng.annotations.Test;
3
4  import static org.mockito.BDDMockito.given;
5  import static org.mockito.Mockito.mock;
6
7  public class OrderServiceTest {
8
9      private CustomerRepository repository;
10
11     @BeforeMethod
12     protected void setUp() {
13         repository = mock(CustomerRepository.class);
14     }
15
16     @Test
17     public void this_test_requires_a_customer() {
18         Customer customer = new Customer();
19         // Set test-specific data on customer
20         given(repository.load(1L)).willReturn(customer);
21         // Test
22         // Assert
23     }
24
25     @Test
26     public void this_test_requires_another_customer() {
27         Customer customer = new Customer();
28         // Set test-specific data on customer
29         given(repository.load(2L)).willReturn(customer);
30         // Test
31         // Assert
32     }
33 }
```

3.3.1.5 Default value

It may happen that the default value needs to be different from null. To achieve this, Mockito offers the mock(Class<T>, Answer). In this case, the Answer parameter will return the default value.

Code 3.11 - Default value returning

```
Customer customer = new Customer();

CustomerRepository repository = mock(CustomerRepository.class,
        (Answer) a -> customer);
assertSame(repository.load(1L), customer);
```

3.3.1.6 Consecutive behavior

Consecutive behavior mimics code that behaves differently after multiple calls *e.g.* returns a value on the first call, and another value on the second.

Usage of consecutive behavior is straightforward: each willReturn() method chained will be called in order during test execution, with the last methods being called afterwards.

Code 3.12 - Consecutive returns

```
CustomerRepository repository = mock(CustomerRepository.class);

given(repository.load(any(Long.class)))
        .willReturn(customer1)
        .willReturn(customer2);

assertSame(repository.load(1L), customer1);
assertSame(repository.load(2L), customer2);
// Same for all calls afterwards
assertSame(repository.load(null), customer2);
```

The previous snippet can be simplified by just using willReturn() with varargs parameters:

Code 3.13 - Simple consecutive returns

```
CustomerRepository repository = mock(CustomerRepository.class);

given(repository.load(any(Long.class))).willReturn(customer1, customer2);

assertSame(repository.load(1L), customer1);
assertSame(repository.load(2L), customer2);
// True for all calls afterwards
assertSame(repository.load(null), customer2);
```

⚷ Mixing returning and exception throwing

Standard return stubs can be mixed and matched with exception-throwing stubs to simulate a wide range of behavior. For example, it can be used to simulate database pool exhaustion limit, having multiple calls returning database connections objects then throwing an exception after some predefined number of calls. However, in this case, the varargs version can not be used.

3.3.1.7 Stubbing summary

The following table summarizes Mockito stubbing behavior, when repository.load() is called after the following setup code with different values:

Table 3.1 - Stubbing examples

Setup code	Parameter value	Returned instance
given(repository.load(1L)).willReturn(customer);	1L	`customer`
	2L	`null`
given(repository.load(any(Integer.class))) .willReturn(customer);	1L	`customer`
	2L	`customer`
given(repository.load(1L) .willReturn(null) .willReturn(customer);	1L	`null`
	1L	`customer`
	2L	`null`
given(repository.load(any(Integer.class))) .willReturn(null) .willReturn(customer);	1L	`null`
	1L	`customer`
	2L	`customer`
given(repository.load(any(Integer.class))) .willReturn(null, customer);	1L	`null`
	1L	`customer`
	2L	`customer`
Customer default = new Customer();		
CustomerRepository repository = mock(CustomerRespository, e -> default);	1L	`default`
	2L	`customer`
given(repository.load(1L)) .willReturn(customer);	3L	`default`

3.3.2 Mocking

Mockito not only provides stubbing capabilities, but also mocking ones. This way, interactions between the mock object and its dependencies can be checked.

 Mockito creates proxies when using the `mock()` method. When a method is called on it, not only does it uses the previously stubbed behavior(s), it also records the method call. The whole mocking feature is built on that. This means that when Mockito method arguments expect an `Object`, it will probably be a mock.

Mockito offers several methods to allow for such checks.

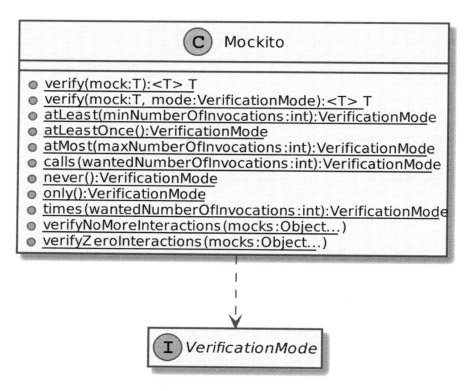

Fig. 3.7 - Mockito mocking API

The entry point into the Mockito mocking API is the `verify()` static method. `verify()` with the mock parameter as a single parameter *i.e.* if no `VerificationMode` is provided, will check for **one single interaction**.

Code 3.14 - Checking a single interaction

```
OrderRepository orderRepo = mock(OrderRepository.class);
CustomerRepository customerRepo = mock(CustomerRepository.class);
ProductRepository productRepo = mock(ProductRepository.class);

OrderService orderService =
        new OrderService(customerRepo, orderRepo, productRepo);

Order order = orderService.order(1L, 1L);

verify(customerRepo).load(1L);
verify(productRepo).load(1L);
verify(orderRepo).save(any(Order.class));
```

We can verify more interaction flavors by passing a VerificationMode to verify() in addition to the mock; Mockito kindly provides static methods to create instances of those:

- atLeast(int) checks for at least *n* interactions
- atLeastOnce() is a specialization of the previous, with *n* = 1
- atMost(int) is the exact opposite of atLeast(int)
- never() is a specialization of the previous, with *n* = 0
- times(int) enforces **exactly** *n* interactions

The preceding snippet can be rendered more lenient by replacing verifying code with the following lines:

Code 3.15 - Checking variable numbers of interaction

```
OrderRepository orderRepo = mock(OrderRepository.class);
CustomerRepository customerRepo = mock(CustomerRepository.class);
ProductRepository productRepo = mock(ProductRepository.class);

OrderService orderService
        = new OrderService(customerRepo, orderRepo, productRepo);

Order order = orderService.order(1L, 1L);

verify(customerRepo).load(1L);
verify(productRepo, atLeastOnce()).load(1L);
verify(orderRepo, atLeastOnce()).save(any(Order.class));
```

Some more methods are available if necessary:

- With `verifyNoMoreInteractions(Object...)`, Mockito checks that the only methods called are the ones that have been `verifyed`:

Code 3.16 - Verifying no more interactions

```
verify(customerRepo).load(1L);
verify(productRepo).load(1L);

verifyNoMoreInteractions(customerRepo, productRepo);
```

The previous snippet will execute successfully, as only `load()` is called on each mock. However, if `orderRepo` is added to the arguments list with no verification, the test will fail as `orderRepo` has its `save()` method called. Should we need to make the test pass again, it is necessary to add `verify(orderRepo).save(any(Order.class))`.

- `only()` checks that the referenced method is the only interaction happening on the mock. It is a shortcut of sorts for combining a standard `verify()` and a `verifyNoMoreInteractions()` in one call. For example, the previous snippet can be replaced by the following:

Code 3.17 - Only

```
verify(customerRepo, only()).load(1L);
verify(productRepo, only()).load(1L);
```

- Finally, checking a mock is not interacted with at all is done with `verifyZeroInteractions(Object...)`

Do not overuse mocking

Mocking is the epitome of white-box testing as it requires knowledge of the underlying interactions between objects. However, white-box testing is more fragile than black-box testing as design is subject to change. Therefore, Mockito verify should be used sparingly.

Besides, not being able to test code without `verify()` is a sure sign of a code smell. Somehow, the existing design might be relying too much on state and side-effects: time to do some Functional Programming oriented refactoring

3.3.3 Partial mocks

Spying is an interesting Mockito feature that enables adding specific behavior on real instances, not just mocks.

Partial mocks are generally considered code smell as it shows that the class may have more than just a single responsibility. However, we are living in an imperfect world, and dealing with either third-party or legacy code is a common occurrence. In this case, it could be desirable to have some methods stubbed, while other would be the "real" methods.

In a greenfield project, be very wary of needing partial mocks though.

Here are several use-cases:

- A Service Locator implementation that also caches objects retrieved from the registry. Only the method that retrieves objects could be stubbed and the real full-fledged cache implementation be used. This brings our SUT closer to real conditions.
- A class sending JMS messages to log its actions. The message sending feature would be stubbed, so tests would not require a full-fledged JMS infrastructure.

Here is a basic example showing partial mock usage:

Code 3.18 - Partial mocking

```
LinkedList list = mock(LinkedList.class);

when(list.getFirst()).thenReturn(Integer.valueOf(0));
when(list.add(any(Integer.class))).thenCallRealMethod();
when(list.get(anyInt())).thenCallRealMethod();
when(list.size()).thenCallRealMethod();

list.add(Integer.valueOf(2));
list.add(Integer.valueOf(2));
list.add(Integer.valueOf(2));

assertEquals(list.size(), 3);
assertEquals(list.get(0), Integer.valueOf(2));
assertNotEquals(list.getFirst(), Integer.valueOf(2));
assertNull(list.getLast());
```

In the above snippet, notice that Mockito is explicitly told which methods should be stubbed, and which ones should use the real underlying behavior. As for standard mocks, unstubbed methods return `null`.

Since telling Mockito to call the real method every time might become quite boring, Mockito also provides the `spy()` method. Whereas `mock()` creates proxies and it is up to the developer to make them full or partial mocks, `spy()` operates on real created instances:

Code 3.19 - Spying

```java
LinkedList<Integer> list = spy(new LinkedList<Integer>());

list.add(Integer.valueOf(2));
list.add(Integer.valueOf(2));
list.add(Integer.valueOf(2));

when(list.getFirst()).thenReturn(Integer.valueOf(0));

assertEquals(list.size(), 3);
assertEquals(list.get(0), Integer.valueOf(2));
assertNotEquals(list.getFirst(), Integer.valueOf(2));
assertEquals(list.getLast(), Integer.valueOf(2));
```

Note the following differences:

1. On one hand, since methods are called on real instances, initialization has to happen on the list before stubbing. Otherwise, `list.getFirst()` will be called on the underlying object and throw a `NoSuchElementException` if the list is empty at that time.
2. On the other hand, Mockito default behavior is to call the underlying method so no explicit call on `thenCallRealMethod()` is necessary: `list.getLast()` returns 2 though it is not stubbed.

 # Do not use the wrapped object

Once Mockito creates the spy, only use the mock in the rest of the code as Mockito records interactions with it and not interactions with the underlying instance. To prevent bugs, the latter should either a) never be referenced or b) only be referenced as a local variable. This means storing it as an attribute of the test class might be a disaster waiting to happen.

3.4 Ready to use Fakes

The previous section covered stubbing and mocking, *i.e.* coding objects to get the exact required behavior. Mocks - respectively stubs, are very useful, but require a lot of effort as their expectation - respectively behavior, has to be explicitly written. Besides, some APIs do not provide default implementations but only interfaces. Creating mocks/stubs when using such APIs may get have a very low ROI and even a negative one; it might cost more to create automated tests using mocks than delivering with no integration-testing harness. This is sadly the case with most of the Java EE APIs. Those include (but are in no way limited to):

- Servlet/Portlet API
- Java Naming and Directory Interface (JNDI)
- Java Messaging Service (JMS)
- JavaMail
- etc.

There are some alternatives to stubbing and mocking:

- Roll-out a dedicated implementation class, usable only for a specific test case. This also requires additional effort, with possible bugs.
- Create a reusable implementation class. This requires even more effort, not only from a development point of view, but also from a version and organizational point of view.
- Reuse an existing implementation library. Most, if not all, of the existing libraries are tightly coupled to a specific application server and dependent on other libraries.
- Finally, some libraries provide reusable mostly test-oriented implementation classes; this is the solution described in this section. It provides several advantages, including increased readability, with reduced test-writing time.

3.4.1 Fakes use-cases

The following are some examples, taken from experience.

 Spring Test is not limited to Spring

In this section, the Fake library used is Spring Test. Although fully integrated with the Spring framework, Spring Test can also be used independently for just the provided Fakes of some important APIs.

3.4.1.1 JNDI

As a quick example, imagine testing a SUT that includes a JNDI Service Locator. The latter must interface with a JNDI directory to return a JDBC Connection Pool as well as cache it to improve performance for consecutive calls. Here are some possible options:

1. Mocking the Locator would move it outside the SUT. Integration between the Locator and other code parts would not be tested, which does not fit our requirement
2. Using a real Java EE 7 container. This will be detailed in *Chapter 9 - Java EE testing*
3. Mocking the Context interacting with the Locator
4. Using a real Context instance. This requires a standalone `javax.naming.Context` implementation

Here is the Service Locator to test:

Code 3.20 - Service Locator to test

```
1    import javax.naming.*;
2    import javax.sql.DataSource;
3
4    public class ServiceLocator {
5
6        private Context context;
7        private String dataSourceJndiLocation;
8        private DataSource dataSource;
9
10       public ServiceLocator(Context context, String dataSourceJndiLocation) {
11           this.context = context;
12           this.dataSourceJndiLocation = dataSourceJndiLocation;
13       }
14
15       public DataSource getDataSource() {
16           if (dataSource == null) {
17               try {
18                   dataSource =
19                       (DataSource) context.lookup(dataSourceJndiLocation);
20               } catch (NamingException e) {
21                   throw new RuntimeException(e);
22               }
23           }
24           return dataSource;
25       }
26   }
```

Note this Service Locator has already been designed to be injectable.

As per the options above, the first mocking implementation could make good use of verify():

Code 3.21 - Mocking with verify

```
Context context = mock(Context.class);
when(context.lookup("dummy")).thenReturn(mock(DataSource.class));

ServiceLocator locator = new ServiceLocator(context, "dummy");
DataSource dataSource = locator.getDataSource();

assertNotNull(dataSource);
assertSame(locator.getDataSource(), dataSource);
verify(context).lookup("dummy");
```

However, this means it is white-box testing and that developers have to know about the nitty-gritty details of the implementation. The test code could be reworked by taking advantage of consecutive behavior, by first returning a DataSource instance, then returning another one:

Code 3.22 - Mocking with consecutive stubbing

```
Context context = mock(Context.class);
when(context.lookup("dummy")).thenReturn(mock(DataSource.class))
                             .thenReturn(mock(DataSource.class));

ServiceLocator locator = new ServiceLocator(context, "dummy");
DataSource dataSource = locator.getDataSource();

assertNotNull(dataSource);
assertSame(locator.getDataSource(), dataSource);
```

This new version is much better regarding white-box testing, but the test code is now harder to read and understand. The best compromise between knowledge of the internals and readability would be to get a working but independent Context implementation.

3.4.1.2 Servlets

Servlets can be tested inside a Servlet container as will be seen in *Chapter 9 - Java EE testing*, or out-of-container.

In the latter case, some test doubles are required:

Table 3.2 - Servlet testing requirements

Class	Methods	Required interface(s)
j.servlet.GenericServlet	init()	j.servlet.ServletConfig
j.servlet.GenericServlet	getServletContext()	j.servlet.ServletContext
j.servlet.ServletRequest	getRequestDispatcher()	j.servlet.RequestDispatcher
j.servlet.Filter	init()	j.servlet.FilterConfig
j.servlet.Filter	doFilter()	j.servlet.ServletRequest j.servlet.ServletResponse j.servlet.FilterChain
j.servlet.http.HttpServlet	doGet() doPost()	j.servlet.http.HttpServletRequest j.servlet.http.HttpServletResponse
j.s.h.HttpServletRequest	getSession()	j.servlet.http.HttpSession

As an example, let us test a servlet that performs the following standard tasks:

1. Gets the ID parameter from the submitted form
2. If the ID is not found, or not a number, throw an exception
3. Load the associated order of the ID that has been found
4. Set the order in the request context
5. Forward to the order JSP with the help of the request dispatcher

Code 3.23 - Servlet to be tested

```
1   import javax.servlet.ServletException;
2   import javax.servlet.http.*;
3   import java.io.IOException;
4
5   public class OrderServlet extends HttpServlet {
6
7       private OrderService service;
8
9       @Override
10      public void init() throws ServletException {
11          // Inject the OrderService somehow
12      }
13
14      @Override
15      public void doGet(HttpServletRequest req, HttpServletResponse resp)
16              throws ServletException, IOException {
17          String pk = req.getParameter("pk");
18          if (pk == null) {
19              throw new ServletException("No ID found");
20          }
21          try {
22              Long id = Long.valueOf(pk);
23              Order order = service.get(id);
24              req.setAttribute("order", order);
25              req.getRequestDispatcher("/WEB-INF/page/order.jsp")
26                  .forward(req, resp);
27          } catch (NumberFormatException e) {
28              throw new ServletException("ID is not a number: "
29                  + e.getMessage());
30          }
31      }
32
33      public void setOrderService(OrderService service) {
34          this.service = service;
35      }
36  }
```

Given this, test cases should be along the following lines:

Table 3.3 - Servlet testing use-cases

Test case	Expectation
No ID parameter	Exception
String ID parameter	Exception
Happy path	Order as request attribute Forward to JSP

The next section highlights how using Fake libraries painlessly resolves our testing issues.

3.4.2 Fakes libraries

Two libraries are at the core of Java EE fakes.

> It may seem strange, but both libraries use the `Mock` prefix instead of `Fake` for the Fake classes they provide.

3.4.2.1 Spring Test

Spring Test is the *de facto* Fake library for the following APIs:

Servlet

Spring Test provides a whole bunch of Fake classes around the Servlet API. In addition to method implementations from their super-interface, Spring Test Fakes offer getters and setters for many underlying properties that cannot be accessed in standard implementations.

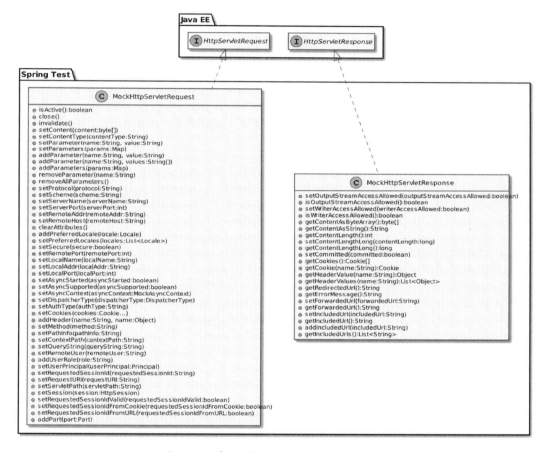

Fig. 3.8 Fake HTTP request and response

In particular, `MockHttpServletRequest` gives us the ability to:

- Append parameters to the request *e.g.* `req.addParameter("id", "12345")`
- Add an user role *e.g.* `req.addUserRole("ADMIN")`
- Set the user identity *e.g.* `req.sertUserPrincipal("admin")`

- Set an existing session, to use Fake one *e.g.*
  `req.setSession(new MockHttpSession())`
- Set the HTTP verb *e.g.* `req.setMethod("GET")`
- Add HTTP headers *e.g.* `req.addHeader("Accept", "text/plain")`

 `setHeader()` sets a specific header while `addHeader()` adds it. The difference is that if the header name already exists, in the former case it **replaces** the value, while in the latter, it adds a header with the **same name** (and the new value). If there is no existing header with the specified name, both have the same behavior.

In turn, `MockHttpServletResponse` enables us to:

- Get the response stream (respectively writer) directly or the content as a byte array (respectively string) *e.g.* `req.getContentAString()`
- Get the forwarded or included URLs *e.g.* `req.getForwardedUrl()`
- Get cookies *e.g.* ‘req.getCookies()

Armed with our newfound knowledge, the previous to-be-tested servlet can be with the following:

Code 3.24 - Servlet test

```
1    import org.springframework.mock.web.*;
2    import org.testng.annotations.*;
3
4    import javax.servlet.ServletException;
5
6    import static org.testng.Assert.*;
7
8    public class OrderServletFakeTest {
9
10       private OrderServlet servlet;
11       private MockHttpServletRequest req;
12       private MockHttpServletResponse resp;
13
14       @BeforeMethod
```

```
15      protected void setUp() {
16
17          servlet = new OrderServlet();
18          OrderService service =
19              new OrderService(null, new OrderRepository(), null);
20          servlet.setOrderService(service);
21
22          req = new MockHttpServletRequest();
23          resp = new MockHttpServletResponse();
24      }
25
26      @Test(expectedExceptions = ServletException.class)
27      public void no_id_should_throw_exception() throws Exception {
28          servlet.doGet(req, resp);
29      }
30
31      @Test(expectedExceptions = ServletException.class)
32      public void bad_type_id_should_throw_ex() throws Exception {
33          req.addParameter("id", "Hello world!");
34          servlet.doGet(req, resp);
35      }
36
37      @Test
38      public void should_set_order_in_request() throws Exception {
39          req.addParameter("id", "1");
40          servlet.doGet(req, resp);
41          Object object = req.getAttribute("order");
42
43          assertNotNull(object);
44          assertTrue(object instanceof Order);
45      }
46
47      @Test
48      public void should_forward_to_order_jsp() throws Exception {
49          req.addParameter("id", "1");
50          servlet.doGet(req, resp);
51
52          assertEquals(resp.getForwardedUrl(),
```

```
53                    "/WEB-INF/page/order.jsp");
54        }
55  }
```

Note this result is obtained without writing a single line of stubbed behavior, with Fakes doing the job of real objects! Other interesting available Fakes include a `MockServletContext` and a `MockRequestDispatcher`.

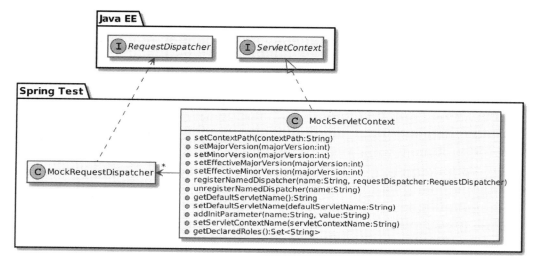

Fig. 3.9 Fake request dispatcher and servlet context

JNDI

Spring Test provides a basic implementation of `javax.naming.Context` with `SimpleNamingContext`: it can be used to bind/unbind resources within the context. The most common use-case is to populate the context during initialization.

`SimpleNamingContextBuilder` is also available as an implementation of `InitialContextFactoryBuilder` should the need arise.

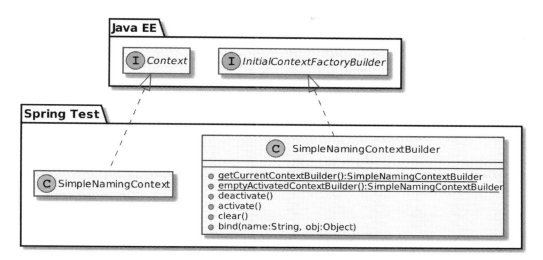

Fig. 3.10 Simple JNDI context

Testing the above Service Locator now becomes a breeze.

Code 3.25 - Faking

```
Context context = new SimpleNamingContext();
context.bind("dummy", new BasicDataSource());

ServiceLocator locator = new ServiceLocator(context, "dummy");
DataSource dataSource = locator.getDataSource();

context.unbind("dummy");

assertNotNull(dataSource);
assertSame(locator.getDataSource(), dataSource);
    }
```

Using this Fake Context with explicit bind() and unbind() removes the need
to code stubbing behavior ourselves.

Portlet

Fakes are readily available for portlets. Since portlets are not really widespread
nowadays, interested readers should have a direct look at the relevant JavaDocs.

3.4.2.2 MockRunner

Spring Test offers a wide range of Fakes, but not on JMS. MockRunner (http://mockrunner.github.io/) is a legacy library providing Fakes for Struts, Servlets, taglibs, Java DataBase Connectivity, Enterprise Java Beans 2.x, Java Messaging System and Java Connector Architecture. It has been recently moved from Sourceforge.net to Github to revive it somewhat.

 As Spring Test has full Pivotal support as part of the Spring framework, it is advised to use Mockrunner only for APIs the former does not provide *i.e.* no Mockrunner Servlet.

Java Messaging System

JMS is a messaging system, offering point-to-point (PtP) and publish-subscribe (P/S) features. As a reminder, the JMS API has two abstraction levels:

- One agnostic toward PtP or P/S with Destination
- The other aimed at them with Queue for the former and Topic for the latter.

JMS 2.0, included in Java EE 7, makes JMS development easier by removing a lot of boilerplate code; unfortunately, at the time of this writing, Mockrunner only provides mocks for the previous 1.x version. Here is a typical JMS component for sending/receiving text messages in a point-to-point model:

Code 3.26 - Send and receive text messages through JMS

```
1    import javax.annotation.Resource;
2    import javax.jms.*;
3
4    import static javax.jms.Session.AUTO_ACKNOWLEDGE;
5
6    public class LegacyJmsComponent {
7
8        @Resource(lookup = "java:comp/env/jms/DefaultConnectionFactory")
9        ConnectionFactory connectionFactory;
10
```

```
11      @Resource(lookup = "java:comp/env/jms/DefaultQueue")
12      Queue queue;
13
14      public void sendMessage(String text) throws JMSException {
15
16          try (Connection connection = connectionFactory.createConnection();
17              Session session =
18                  connection.createSession(false, AUTO_ACKNOWLEDGE)) {
19              MessageProducer producer = session.createProducer(queue);
20              TextMessage message = session.createTextMessage(text);
21              producer.send(message);
22          } catch (JMSException e) {
23              throw new RuntimeException(e);
24          }
25      }
26
27      public String receiveMessage() {
28
29          try (Connection connection = connectionFactory.createConnection();
30              Session session =
31                  connection.createSession(false, AUTO_ACKNOWLEDGE)) {
32              MessageConsumer consumer = session.createConsumer(queue);
33              Message message = consumer.receive();
34              if (message instanceof TextMessage) {
35                  return ((TextMessage) message).getText();
36              }
37              throw new RuntimeException("Not a text message");
38          } catch (JMSException e) {
39              throw new RuntimeException(e);
40          }
41      }
42  }
```

Mockrunner provides Fakes for every JMS interface, yet some are more important than others; in particular, given the previous code design, Fakes for ConnectionFactory and Queue are required.

For ConnectionFactory, Mockrunner offers a MockConnectionFactory imple-
menting both QueueConnectionFactory and TopicConnectionFactory.
MockConnectionFactory gives read access to its connections pool. Its
MockQueueConnectionFactory (respectively MockTopicConnectionFactory) sub-
class does the same while narrowing the returned connection to be of type
MockQueueConnection (resp. MockTopicConnection).

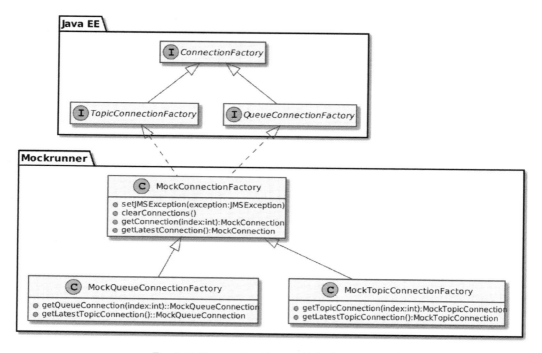

Fig. 3.11 Connection Factory Fake hierarchy

For Queue, Mockrunner provides a MockDestination that implements JMS
Destination. With MockDestination, message instances can easily be added
and get to the destination. Note that its subclasses do not have more features,
beyond the standard JMS API methods.

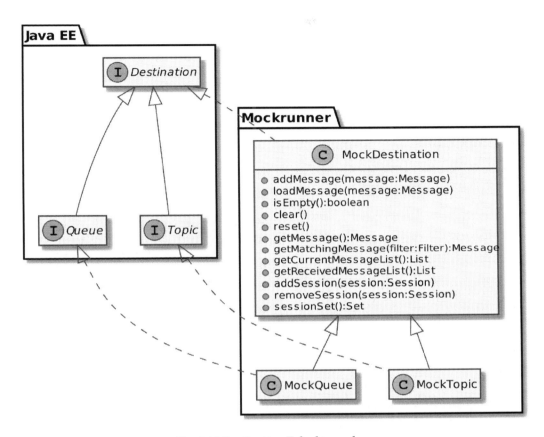

Fig. 3.12 Destination Fake hierarchy

Last but not least, Mockrunner makes Fakes available for Message and every one of its sub interface. This is interesting when testing reading/peeking messages so we can add test messages in the destination.

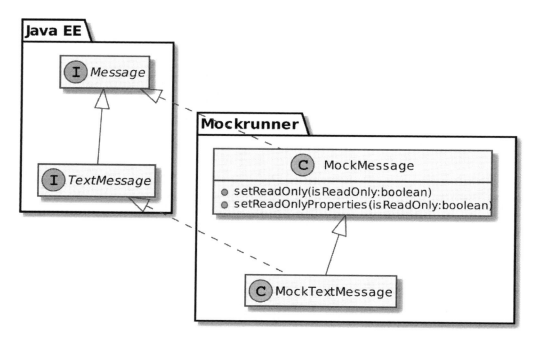

Fig. 3.13 Message Fake hierarchy

With Mockrunner, testing our previous code becomes much easier: the required
`ConnectionFactory` and `Queue` dependencies can be set with Fakes and Fake
messages can be added to the queue to test `receiveMessage()`.

Code 3.27 - JMS testing using Fakes

```
1    import com.mockrunner.jms.*;
2    import com.mockrunner.mock.jms.*;
3    import org.testng.annotations.*;
4
5    import javax.jms.*;
6
7    import static org.testng.Assert.*;
8
9    public class LegacyJmsComponentTest {
10
11       private LegacyJmsComponent jmsComponent;
```

```
12          private MockQueue q;
13
14          @BeforeMethod
15          protected void setUp() {
16              jmsComponent = new LegacyJmsComponent();
17              q = new MockQueue("dummy");
18
19              jmsComponent.connectionFactory = new MockConnectionFactory(
20                  new DestinationManager(), new ConfigurationManager());
21              jmsComponent.queue = q;
22          }
23
24          @Test
25          public void send_message_should_send_a_single_message_in_q()
26                  throws JMSException {
27              jmsComponent.sendMessage("Hello world!");
28              Message message = q.getMessage();
29
30              assertNotNull(message);
31              assertTrue(message instanceof TextMessage);
32
33              String text = ((TextMessage) message).getText();
34
35              assertEquals(text, "Hello world!");
36              assertNull(q.getMessage());
37          }
38
39          @Test(expectedExceptions = RuntimeException.class)
40          public void receive_message_should_throw_when_no_messages_in_q() {
41              jmsComponent.receiveMessage();
42          }
43
44          @Test
45          public void receive_message_should_receive_message_in_q()
46                  throws JMSException {
47              q.addMessage(new MockTextMessage("Hello"));
48              q.addMessage(new MockTextMessage("world!"));
49
```

```
50          assertEquals(jmsComponent.receiveMessage(), "Hello");
51          assertEquals(jmsComponent.receiveMessage(), "world!");
52      }
53  }
```

3.5 Summary

This chapter first covered how Dependency Injection techniques used for Unit Testing can be used again for Integration Testing. It leads to a description of the different flavors of Test Doubles:

- Dummies
- Stubs
- Mocks
- Fakes

Regarding stubs and mocks, Mockito is the framework of choice as it makes it very easy to create both. On the fakes side, two libraries to ease testing were described, Mockrunner for JMS and Spring Test for the rest of the Java EE API.

The next chapter will detail how integration tests can be automated and the best way to achieve that.

4. Automated testing

Tests, whether unit tests or integration tests, are no good if they require a lengthy and manual process to set up and execute. A whole approach known as Continuous Integration enables this automated testing lifecycle.

4.1 Continuous integration

Continous integration (http://en.wikipedia.org/wiki/Continuous_integration)(also known as CI) is the process of building software from the code merged from the contribution of all developers. Building includes:

- Compiling
- Different flavors of testing
- Optionally, packaging

Commonly-used continuous integration platforms include Atlassian Bamboo, Hudson CI and Jenkins CI. However, each would require a dedicated book: interested readers are welcome to search for one as plenty exist.

Continuous integration is leveraged by automated build tools, such as Ant, Maven and Gradle.

4.2 Automated build tools

Build automation has been around for quite some time, as having repeatable builds is at the core of a software engineer's job. In the beginning, people used Make files as a lesser evil, then Apache Ant managed to bring platform-independent build management through Java.

However, Ant had one big flaw: each build file was custom made. Each time one walked into a new project, one had to get acquainted with its build file specifics.

4.2.1 Maven

Apache Maven has been around for quite some time and it is well beyond the scope of this book. This section will be restricted to the domain of testing only.

Testing frameworks seen in *Chapter 2 - Developer testing tools* such as JUnit and TestNG are integrated with Maven out-of-the-box. As Maven is based on a plugin architecture, this integration is achieved through the Maven Surefire plugin.

4.2.1.1 Surefire basics

In short, any test following these rules will be executed by Surefire:

- Test classes must be located inside the `src/test/java` folder of the Maven project (or module)
- Test class names must either:
    - start with `Test` *e.g.* `TestCustomerService`
    - end with `Test` *e.g.* `CustomerServiceTest`
    - end with `TestCase` *e.g.* `CustomerServiceTestCase`

 As with many defaults in Maven, this convention can be overwitten by configuring the Project Object Model (POM) file. It requires to update the `include` tag of the Surefire plugin.

- Test cases must not be disabled by its framework specifics (`@Ignore` for Junit or `@Test(enabled = false)` for TestNG)

This means that all tests will be executed, regardless of their exact nature - unit or integration. Having both unit and integration tests executed at the same time has 3 major drawbacks:

1. Unit testing is used to get quick feedback before a commit to validate everything works as expected. By mixing in integration tests which are slower, the feedback loop is also slower. At best, it decreases productivity, at worst, developers decline to launch tests before committing.
2. Integration tests tend to be more fragile than unit tests. Having a build fail because of a setup error is incredibly damaging for developers: as above, this leads to make them ignoring testing their code.
3. Finally, most continuous integration jobs include some degree of code coverage: it is not enough to test code, it is not even enough to know how much code is tested, the goal is to follow the code coverage trend from day-to-day. However, unit code coverage and integration test coverage are very different beasts: they should be covered by different metrics.

4.2.1.2 Failsafe to the rescue

Segregating between unit and integration tests is very simple, thanks to another of Maven's plugins - Failsafe. As the name implies, Failsafe is a complete clone of Surefire save 3 important differences:

1. By default, test class names must either start or end with IT (for Integration Test) or end with ITCase *e.g.* ITCustomerService, CustomerServiceIT and CustomerServiceITCase

    Stick to convention While it is possible to override the default naming conventions, and even though they might not suite your taste, doing so will only result maintainers spending more time to understand your intent. Stick as much as possible to Maven's conventions.

2. The Maven lifecycle for unit testing provide the test phase, while it provides multiple phases for integration tests:

- pre-integration-test
- integration-test
- post-integration-test
- verify

Note that the *pre-* and *post-* phases are rarely used (if at all).

3. The Failsafe plugin is **not** bound to any Maven lifecycle phase by default. Its goals have to be bound explicitly to each respective phase in the POM. This can be done in the `<plugins>` section of the POM file itself:

Code 4.1 - Simple Failsafe integration

```
1  <project ...>
2      <modelVersion>4.0.0</modelVersion>
3      <groupId>ch.frankel.integrationtest</groupId>
4      <artifactId>automation</artifactId>
5      <version>1.0.0</version>
6      <build>
7          <plugins>
8              <plugin>
9                  <artifactId>maven-failsafe-plugin</artifactId>
10                 <version>2.17</version>
11                 <executions>
12                     <execution>
13                         <id>integration-test</id>
14                         <goals>
15                             <goal>integration-test</goal>
16                         </goals>
17                         <phase>integration-test</phase>
18                     </execution>
19                     <execution>
20                         <id>verify</id>
21                         <goals>
22                             <goal>verify</goal>
23                         </goals>
24                         <phase>verify</phase>
25                     </execution>
26                 </executions>
27             </plugin>
```

```
28          </plugins>
29        </build>
30    </project>
```

As `integration-test` and `verify` are mostly the only one used, only those are bound. Alternatively, it can also be achieved by using the `<pluginManagement>` section of one of its parent(s) **and** declaring usage of the plugin in the project's POM:

Code 4.2 - Failsafe integration within a parent POM

```
1    <project ...>
2        <modelVersion>4.0.0</modelVersion>
3        <groupId>ch.frankel.integrationtest</groupId>
4        <artifactId>integrationtest</artifactId>
5        <packaging>pom</packaging>
6        <version>1.0.0</version>
7        <modules>
8            <module>automation</module>
9        </modules>
10       <build>
11           <pluginManagement>
12               <plugins>
13                   <plugin>
14                       <artifactId>maven-failsafe-plugin</artifactId>
15                       <version>2.17</version>
16                       <executions>
17                           <execution>
18                               <id>integration-test</id>
19                               <goals>
20                                   <goal>integration-test</goal>
21                               </goals>
22                               <phase>integration-test</phase>
23                           </execution>
24                           <execution>
25                               <id>verify</id>
26                               <goals>
27                                   <goal>verify</goal>
```

```
28                              </goals>
29                              <phase>verify</phase>
30                          </execution>
31                      </executions>
32                  </plugin>
33              </plugins>
34          </pluginManagement>
35      </build>
36  </project>
```

At this point, calling `mvn integration-test` will trigger the `integration-test` goal of the Failsafe plugin, thus ensuring all integration tests that follow the above naming conventions will be executed.

4.2.1.3 Managing brittleness

Integration tests can be divided into two different groups:

- On one side, there are tests whose dependencies are taken care of by the test itself *e.g.* through mocks or fakes. As such, a test failure can only be blamed on the code itself.
- On the other side, there are tests dependent on the environment. Such tests will fail if a dependency is not available during test execution: those tests are particularly brittle and must be handled in a specific way.

While the brittleness of these latter tests should make usage of them a rare occurence if at all, one might want to test integration of the system as a whole inside its ecosystem. In such a case, neither mocking nor faking can really help. This has some serious consequences.

Dependency on infrastructure resources means builds will sometimes break for reasons unrelated to your code. If that happens during a standard build, this is not such a big problem; however, during a planned release, this is bound to create some frustration. If such red herrings happen more than once in stressful conditions, sooner or later, guilty tests will be disabled... then probably deleted. In order to address this issue, there are a couple of possible solutions - but before considering them, here is how things work.

In the POM above, notice that two different goals on two different lifecycle phases have been set up: the `integration-test` goal only runs integration tests (and creates reports) while the `verify` goal verifies there has been no failure. The options are the following:

1. The first option is to unbind the `verify` goal from its corresponding lifecycle phase. This way, `verify` will never get called... and the build will never break. This is an extreme option, like disabling a failed test to make the build pass.

2. One can also set the `testFailureIgnore` parameter of the `verify` plugin to `true`. This can be done either in the POM or on the command-line:

   ```
   mvn verify -DtestFailureIgnore=true
   ```

3. Another solution is to move integration tests into a dedicated module which is not listed as a module of the parent POM. Therefore, the standard build will run its course with no interference from integration tests, while integration tests will still run.

    In this case, do not forget to run the module with the integration tests

4. The reason why tests sometimes fail is that some (but hopefully not all) tests might be dependent on environment resources (*e.g.* database, mail and so on). The best option is to decide what to do for each test : fake those dependencies (as will be detailed in the *Chapter 5 - Infrastructure Resources Integration* so as to be completely decoupled from the infrastructure or move the test into a dedicated project as in option 3 above.

The following screenshot displays the final structure:

Fig. 4.1 - Maven layout with fragile integration tests

1. Includes self-contained tests, whether unit or integration
2. Includes fragile integration tests dependent on the environment

Given this structure, here is a summary of all possible command lines and their effect depending on their location:

Table 4.1 - Command-line examples

Directory	Command	Effect
main	`mvn test`	Runs `UnitTest` and breaks the build if it fails
main	`mvn integration-test`	1. Runs `UnitTest` and breaks the build if it fails 2. Runs `SelfContainedIT` but does not break the build if it fails
main	`mvn verify`	1. Runs `UnitTest` and breaks the build if it fails 2. Runs `SelfContainedIT` and also breaks the build if it fails
integrationtests	`mvn test`	Does nothing (as there are no unit tests)
integrationtests	`mvn integration-test`	Runs `FragileDependentIT` but does not break the build if it fails
integrationtests	`mvn integration-test`	Runs `FragileDependentIT` and breaks the build if it fails
myproject	`mvn test`	Runs `UnitTest` and breaks the build if it fails
myproject	`mvn integration-test`	1. Runs `UnitTest` and breaks the build if it fails 2. Runs `SelfContainedIT` but does not break the build if it fails 3. Runs `FragileDependentIT` but does not break the build if it fails
myproject	`mvn verify`	1. Runs `UnitTest` and breaks the build if it fails 2. Runs `SelfContainedIT` and also breaks the build if it fails 3. Runs `FragileDependentIT` and also breaks the build if it fails

4.2.1.4 Easier dependency management with BOMs

Bill of Material POMs (BOMs) are not specific to Integration Testing but help tremendously in managing depedencies and aim to resolve the following problem.

In Maven, parent POMs are used for many interesting things, in particular managing dependency versions and scopes across all its children. However, Maven limits a POM to a single (optional) parent POM. Therefore, all data regarding dependencies must be put in one of the ancestors. Problems begin to arise when more than one "provider" offers a parent POM as only one can be inherited.

A BOM is basically a library of a dependencies data: it is designed as a normal POM, with a packaging type of pom that has only a <dependencyManagement> section where scope and version are set:

Code 4.3 - BOM sample

```xml
1   <?xml version="1.0" encoding="UTF-8"?>
2   <project ...>
3       <groupId>com.integrationtest</groupId>
4       <artifactId>bom-example</artifactId>
5       <version>1.0</version>
6       <packaging>pom</packaging>
7       <dependencyManagement>
8           <dependencies>
9               <dependency>
10                  <groupId>com.integrationtest</groupId>
11                  <artifactId>module-A</artifactId>
12                  <version>2.1</version>
13              </dependency>
14              <dependency>
15                  <groupId>com.integrationtest</groupId>
16                  <artifactId>module-B</artifactId>
17                  <version>3.2</version>
18              </dependency>
19          </dependencies>
20      </dependencyManagement>
21  </project>
```

BOM users then declare this dependency in the standard <dependencies> section:

Code 4.4 - BOM usage example

```
1   <?xml version="1.0" encoding="UTF-8"?>
2   <project ...>
3       <groupId>com.integrationtest</groupId>
4       <artifactId>bom-user</artifactId>
5       <version>0.99</version>
6       <dependencies>
7           <dependency>
8               <groupId>com.integrationtest</groupId>
9               <artifactId>bom-example</artifactId>
10              <version>1.0</version>
11              <type>pom</type>
12              <scope>import</scope>
13          </dependency>
14          <dependency>
15              <groupId>com.integrationtest</groupId>
16              <artifactId>module-B</artifactId>
17          </dependency>
18      </dependencies>
19  </project>
```

In the previous POM, the `com.integrationtest:module-A` dependency will be added on the compile classpath in version 2.1. More detailed information on this feature can be found in the Maven documentation: http://maven.apache.org/guides/introduction/introduction-to-dependency-mechanism.html#Importing_Dependencies

Available BOMs

BOM are generally offered by frameworks big enough to be designed into modules. At the moment, they include:

- Spring, seen in *Chapter 7*
- Arquillian, seen in *Chapter 9*
- Hibernate (http://hibernate.org/)
- RESTEasy (http://resteasy.jboss.org/)
- WildFly (http://www.wildfly.org/), formerly known as JBoss Application Server
- Jersey (https://jersey.java.net/)

4.2.2 Gradle

Gradle (http://www.gradle.org/) is another build tool that uses the Groovy language and thus runs on the JVM. While less used than Maven, it is useful for use-cases where Maven is too rigid. For example, Maven's structure pushes developers to have a single project for each binary, and makes it hard to do otherwise. Nonetheless, many projects aimed at the Android platform prefer to have a single project but a dedicated binary for each targeted device with a screen size so as to have lighter binaries.

Code 4.5 - A simple Gradle build file

```
1   apply plugin: 'java'
2
3   sourceCompatibility = 1.8
4   version = '1.0'
5
6   repositories {
7       mavenCentral()
8   }
9
10  dependencies {
```

```
11      testCompile group: 'testng', name: 'testng', version: '6.8.8'
12  }
```

Gradle has some similarities with Maven: by default, it has the same structure (src/main and src/test) and it supports JUnit and TestNG out-of-the-box. The biggest difference between Gradle and Maven however, is that instead of a declarative XML-based POM, it has a Groovy code build file aptly named build.gradle.

Also, regarding Integration Testing, **Gradle has no integration-test task by default**. Fortunately, something similar can be achieved quite easily in each Gradle build file with a new Gradle integrationTest task. Here are the basic requirements for such a task, feel free to add your own:

- The existing test task must only run test files following the Maven Surefire plugin defaults (start with Test or end with Test or TestCase)
- The new integrationTest task must only run test files following the Maven Failsafe plugin defaults (start with IT or end with IT or ITCase)
- The new integrationTest task must only run after the test task
- Both tasks should run TestNG tests

Code 4.6 - The same Gradle build file including integration tests

```
1   apply plugin: 'java'
2
3   sourceCompatibility = 1.8
4   version = '1.0'
5
6   repositories {
7       mavenCentral()
8   }
9
10  dependencies {
11      testCompile group: 'testng', name: 'testng', version: '6.8.8'
12  }
13
14  test {
```

```
15        include '**/Test*.java'
16        include '**/*Test.java'
17        include '**/*TestCase.java'
18    }
19
20    task integrationTest(type: Test, dependsOn: "test") << {
21        include '**/IT*.java'
22        include '**/*IT.java'
23        include '**/*ITCase.java'
24    }
```

Lines 14-18

Configures the standard test task to include only requested patterns. Please check http://www.gradle.org/docs/current/dsl/org.gradle.api.tasks.testing.Test. html#org.gradle.api.tasks.testing.Test for more information.

Line 20

Adds a new integrationTest task, of type Test and depending on task test

Lines 21-24

As per test above, configure requested patterns

Thanks to this Gradle build file, Maven's option #4 above for managing brittleness can be used.

At this point, launching the integration tests is achieved with the following command-line:

```
gradle integrationTest
```

4.3 Summary

This chapter described how to used build tools such as Maven and Gradle to run tests in an automated build process. Specifics about each build tool were detailed, such as the differences between integration-test and verify for Maven, or how to implement an integrationTest task in Gradle.

The next chapter will describe how components interacting with infrastructure resources can also benefit from Fakes.

5. Infrastructure Resources Integration

Applications are seldom found in the void: they interact with resources such as file systems, databases, SMTP servers, FTP servers and the like. Infrastructure integration refers to how application interactions with those resources can be tested and validated. While mocks or fakes can be used in place of infrastructure resources, they will not help validate the behavior of those resources.

This chapter covers strategies and tools to achieve testing resources in the following domains:

- System Time
- Filesystem
- Databases
- Mail servers
- FTP servers

Similar strategies can be used for other resource types. However, Web Services integration will be the subject of the next chapter given its scope.

5.1 Common resource integration testing techniques

This section describes techniques that enable and ease Integration Testing resources integration.

5.1.1 No hard-coded resource reference

Most infrastructure resources have something in common: they can be located through a unique identifier and offer a set of commands to be called. The following table displays some resources with an example identifier:

Table 5.1 - Resource identifiers sample

Resource	Identifier	Example
Relational DataBase Management System	Java Database Connectivity URL	`jdbc:mysql://localhost:3306/myapp`
SMTP server	Domain	`smtp.gmail.com`
FTP server	URL	`ftp://ftp.ietf.cnri.reston.va.us/`

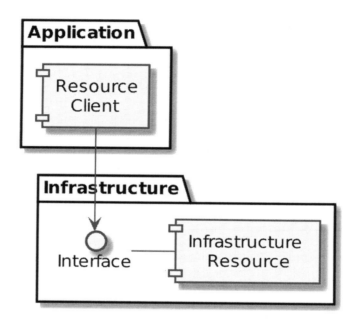

Fig. 5.1 - Resource usage modeling

To enable testing, those URLs and domains should neither be hard-coded nor packaged into the deployed application in any way, so as to be able to change them without redeploying.

Java EE JNDI resources

Java EE application servers already provide references on resources through their Java Naming and Directory Interface (JNDI) resources tree:

- Developers reference resources through their JNDI locations, that are compiled and thus stay the same throughout different environments
- Server administrators bind physical resources to those locations, and of course those resources are different from environment to environment. For more information on JNDI, please check the JNDI Oracle trail (http://docs.oracle.com/javase/tutorial/jndi/).

In pure Java, not hard-coding resource references is typically achieved by using Properties (http://docs.oracle.com/javase/7/docs/api/java/util/Properties.html) file(s). Properties are plain key value pairs, formatted as key=value. This is a basic example of reading such a file:

Code 5.1 - Reading from a Properties file

```java
import java.io.*;
import java.util.Properties;
import java.util.logging.Logger;

public class LoadProperties {

    private static final Logger LOGGER =
            Logger.getLogger(LoadProperties.class.getName());
    private Properties properties = new Properties();

    public LoadProperties() {
        File file = new File("/path/to/file.properties");
        try (FileInputStream stream = new FileInputStream(file)) {
            properties.load(stream);
        } catch (FileNotFoundException e) {
            LOGGER.severe("Properties file does not exist");
```

```
17              throw new RuntimeException(e);
18          } catch (IOException e) {
19              LOGGER.warning("Could not close Properties file");
20          }
21      }
22
23      public String getValueOf(String key) {
24          return properties.getProperty(key);
25      }
26  }
```

 Adding an indirection level

In the previous sample, the Properties file path is hard-coded. In most cases though, a second indirection layer is required to have a path dependent on the context (testing, development, production, etc.). This becomes a requirement when the developer machines Operating System is different from the deployed environments OS. There are many ways to achieve this, but the most common way is through a System Property: the Virtual Machine is started with an agreed-upon System parameter *e.g.* -Dapp.properties=/path/to/file.properties.

In this case, the following snippet should replace line 13 above:

```
12  String path = System.getProperty("app.properties",
13                              "/default/file.properties");
14  File file = new File(path);
```

5.1.2 Setting up and cleaning data

When integration testing resources have state (*e.g.* filesystems, databases, JMS queues, etc), data sometimes has to be set up. There are two different cases:

- Repository data that is to be set up and never (or very rarely) removed. For example, a list of countries

- Contextual data that provides data to be manipulated. For example, emails to test the POP3 receiving feature

Most of the time, sample data is set up before running tests and all data cleaned after the run. But, if a test fails, and the resource state has been wiped clean, there is no clue as to the reason why it failed. Thus, it is much more convenient to **first clear data then set sample data during initialization** and do nothing during clean up (at least nothing regarding data) to keep the state if needed.

5.2 System Time integration

Time-dependent components are among the hardest ones to test, since time is something that cannot easily be mocked/faked/stubbed for testing purposes. Fortunately, there are a couple of answers to this:

Manually

Manually changing the system time is a possible option when testing manually. However, this is completely out of the question in regard to automated testing.

Compatible design

In Java, time usage is based on `System.currentTimeMillis()` but there is no counterpart programmatic setter for this getter. Directly using this API couples the calling code to the system clock. In order to improve testability, the call should be embedded inside an abstraction, with a default implementation using `System.currentTimeMillis()`. Here is a proposed design:

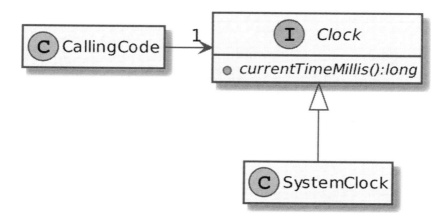

Fig. 5.2 - Design compatible with testing

This way, the Clock can be replaced by a Mock in tests.

Joda Time

Joda Time is a library that aims to provide a better Date class, but offers a whole API for time management (for happy Java 8 users, it is integrated into the java.time package). It also offers a wrapper around System.currentTimeMillis() out-of-the-box: by default, DateTimeUtils.currentTimeMillis() delegates to the former. However, unlike the native API, Joda Time's can be plugged with alternative implementations.

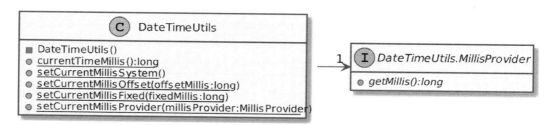

Fig. 5.3 - Joda Time API for system time testing

Alternative implementations include:

- A fixed time implementation with DateTimeUtils.setCurrentMillisFixed(long fixedMillis)

- `DateTimeUtils.setCurrentMillisOffset(long offsetMillis)` provides an offset time implementation *e.g.* a fixed time difference with the system time.

Getting back to using the system time is achieved by calling `DateTimeUtils.setCurrentMillisSystem()`. If the provided alternative are not enough, a custom `MillisProvider` implementation can be developed.

 ## Not Invented Here syndrom

Using design option #2 above shows off one's design skills and lets different classes use different system times. However, such manual development takes time and brings nothing to the table in comparison to Joda Time. Besides, requirements to have different system times is not common (to say the least). In most cases, going the Joda Time way is the most worthwile; chances are it will already be used in the project anyway.

5.3 Filesystem integration

Some applications expect file(s) as input(s) and produce file(s) as output(s); these are commonly known as **Batch**-type applications. The goal of this section is to describe how to provide the former and to assert the existence and content of the latter.

Before Java 7, files were handled through the `java.io.File` class. Here is a class dedicated to reading from and writing to files using this legacy class.

Code 5.2 - Legacy file reading/writing features

```
1    import java.io.*;
2
3    public class LegacyFileComponent {
4
5        public void writeContent(String content, File file) {
6
7            if (file.isDirectory()) {
8                throw new RuntimeException("Cannot write content to directory");
9            }
10
11           if (!file.exists()) {
12               try {
13                   file.createNewFile();
14               } catch (IOException e) {
15                   throw new RuntimeException(e);
16               }
17           } else if (!file.canWrite()) {
18               throw new RuntimeException("Cannot write to file");
19           }
20
21           try (FileWriter writer = new FileWriter(file)) {
22               writer.write(content);
23               writer.flush();
24           } catch (IOException e) {
25               throw new RuntimeException(e);
26           }
27       }
28
29       public String readContent(File file) {
30
31           if (file.isDirectory()) {
32               throw new RuntimeException("Cannot read directory content");
33           }
34
35           if (!file.canRead()) {
36               throw new RuntimeException("Cannot read file");
```

```
37              }
38
39          try (FileReader reader = new FileReader(file)) {
40              StringBuffer buffer = new StringBuffer();
41              int ch;
42              while ((ch = reader.read()) != -1) {
43                  buffer.append((char) ch);
44              }
45              return buffer.toString();
46          } catch (IOException e) {
47              throw new RuntimeException(e);
48          }
49      }
50  }
```

Given this code, testing requires the injection of File instances. Since File depends on the file system, referencing a real file is necessary. This is possible by using the java.io.tmpdir system property that points to the system temporary directory (it should be writable on most if not all systems with no privileges). Testing code would look something like the following:

Code 5.3 - Testing legacy File

```
1   @Test
2   public void read_file_should_retrieve_content() throws Exception {
3
4       String dir = System.getProperty("java.io.tmpdir");
5       File file = new File(dir, "dummy.txt");
6
7       file.createNewFile();
8       FileOutputStream fos = new FileOutputStream(file);
9       fos.write("Hello world!".getBytes());
10
11      String content = legacy.readContent(file);
12
13      assertEquals(content, "Hello world!");
14  }
```

Things are easier since Java 7, as the API offers the new `java.nio.file.Path` interface to provide an abstraction over the file system. The previous component can be replaced with this one while still keeping the same test code. Just replace the `File` parameter with a `Path`, this is easily achieved with `file.getPath()`.

Code 5.4 - New file reading/writing features

```java
import java.io.IOException;
import java.nio.file.*;
import java.util.List;

public class NewestFileComponent {

    public void writeContent(String content, Path path) {

        if (!Files.exists(path)) {
            try {
                Files.createFile(path);
            } catch (IOException e) {
                throw new RuntimeException(e);
            }
        }

        if (Files.isDirectory(path)) {
            throw new RuntimeException("Cannot write into directory");
        }

        if (!Files.isWritable(path)) {
            throw new RuntimeException("No write permissions");
        }

        try {
            Files.write(path, content.getBytes());
        } catch (IOException e) {
            throw new RuntimeException(e);
        }
    }
}
```

```
32    public String readContent(Path path) {
33
34        if (!Files.exists(path)) {
35            throw new RuntimeException("File doesn't exist");
36        }
37
38        if (Files.isDirectory(path)) {
39            throw new RuntimeException("Cannot read from a directory");
40        }
41
42        if (!Files.isReadable(path)) {
43            throw new RuntimeException("No read permissions");
44        }
45
46        try {
47            List<String> lines = Files.readAllLines(path);
48            StringBuffer buffer = new StringBuffer();
49            lines.stream().forEach(line -> buffer.append(line));
50            return buffer.toString();
51        } catch (IOException e) {
52            throw new RuntimeException(e);
53        }
54    }
55 }
```

 ## Stubbing files

Stubbing file behavior when using either File or Path is possible, but it achieves nothing since the behavior that needs to be tested is the one to be stubbed.

5.4 Database integration

Different Java projects use various persistence strategies (SQL vs NoSQL), different database vendors and different ways to access their persistence store(s).

In the SQL realm, RDBMS are standardized enough to provide a common abstraction layer so there are many more ways to access them from Java. From the oldest to the most recent, these are:

- Plain old Java DataBase Connectivity, JDBC
- EJB 2.x Entity Beans, CMP & BMP
- Java Data Objects (http://db.apache.org/jdo/index.html), JDO
- Java Persistence API (http://docs.oracle.com/javaee/5/tutorial/doc/bnbpz.html), JPA
- Hibernate (http://hibernate.org/orm/)
- EclipseLink (http://projects.eclipse.org/projects/rt.eclipselink)
- MyBatis (http://mybatis.github.io/mybatis-3/)
- Spring Data (http://projects.spring.io/spring-data/)
- jOOQ (http://www.jooq.org/)

 Spring Data and Hibernate OGM are the frameworks that bridge the traditional SQL realm with newer NoSQL datastores.

In general, for NoSQL solutions, the vendor offers both the store and the connector(s) to access it. For example, MongoDB (http://www.mongodb.org/) is fully under the vendor control and consists of the persistence store itself, a command-line interface and a Java driver. For the record, there is also a third-party Jongo (http://jongo.org/) driver.

5.4.1 SQL Database integration

Regarding Database Integration Testing, a benefit of SQL standardization is that the following section applies to any database product.

5.4.1.1 Datastore environment strategies

Integration Testing with a data store cannot use a single shared instance as is the case for deployed environments (Development, Q&A, Production, etc.). There is probably more than one developer, and they each need to test on their own database, without the possibility of stepping on their colleagues toes. This requires each developer to have a dedicated database. Basically, there are 3 different strategies to address this:

In-memory database

In-memory databases are dedicated data stores, running in-memory on the developer machine. Available in-memory databases include Apache Derby (http://docs.oracle.com/javadb/10.8.3.0/getstart/index.html) (also released by Oracle under the name "Java DB"), HSQLDB (http://hsqldb.org/) and H2 (http://www.h2database.com/). In-memory DBs greatest advantage are their ability to be set up (and discarded) quickly and easily, thus making **test execution completely independent from infrastructure**.

Using a in-memory database for testing means handling the mismatch between the testing DB and the deployed DB(s) capabilities. At a minimum, the portion of SQL syntax used should stick to the syntax supported by both, which usually limits development options.

All above referenced in-memory databases also support persistent storage on the file system. Then, in case of failure, the DB state can be checked after test execution. Since it is very easy to configure - with the only require- ment a change in the JDBC URL - there is no reason not to use this. For example, H2 persistent file storage can be configured with a URL such as `jdbc:h2:[<path>]/<databaseName>`.

H2 competitive advantages

In most cases, H2 should be the preferred in-memory database:

1. It supports a compatibility mode that makes it understand some proprietary SQL idioms from major RDBMS vendors. Although this has to be checked on the deployed DB as early as possible, it relaxes somewhat constraints on the SQL syntax used.
2. Its JAR contains an embedded webapp that allows to connect to any JDBC-compatible database, complete with schema browsing and interactive querying.
3. Finally, H2 documentation is top-notch. Just have a look at http://www.h2database.com/html/features.html

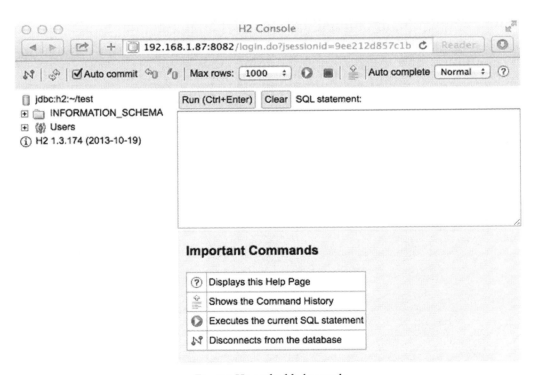

Fig. 5.4 H2 embedded console

Persistent or in-memory?

So called in-memory databases can run entirely in memory **or** be persisted on the filesystem. Each option has its advantages: with in-memory, there is no need to clean up the database at the beginning of a new test suite, while the persisten option enables to check the database state.

Local database

With a local database, each developer installs a copy of the deployed RDBMS on his local development machine. This strategy guarantees 100% compatibility with the deployed platform, at the cost of always keeping the local software version synchronized with the deployed one. Moreover, software installation becomes a prerequisite as it cannot be automated (or very painfully) during application build.

Licensing for local installation

With Open Source RDBMS *e.g.* MySQL or PostgreSQL, an unlimited number of copies on an unlimited number of machines can be installed free of charge. This is not the case with commercial products such as Oracle. The good news: Oracle provides Oracle Database Express Edition *aka* Oracle XE, a database that can be freely installed on all developer machines; the bad news, it is *based* on the commercial product but is not the same product and therefore compatibility issues have to be tested (albeit to a lesser extent than with another different database).

Single remote database per developer

This strategy is about creating a dedicated database per application and per developer. Following this strategy mandates that the Database Administrator(s) has to create one database per developer on the deployed platform (in general, the deployed development environment) and each developer to use it for their tests. It is the best strategy to ensure the exact same behavior during testing **and** in production. On the downside, it either require developers to have admin rights on a database or a working process enrolling the DBA.

Oracle schemas

Oracle Database allows you to have more than one schema under the same JDBC URL. When using it, instead of having one database per developer it is advised to use one dedicated schema instead - this is much easier to set up.

Choosing one strategy over the others really is a matter of context. If you enjoy a good relationship with the DBAs in the organization and plenty of disk space is available, you should probably go for a single remote database. If the project is Open Source and anyone can get the sources and execute the tests, you should use in-memory databases.

All the aforementioned strategies require the same flexibility: to be able to configure the mapping between a developer and a URL (or a schema) during test runs. There are different ways to achieve this, but the primart way should be to use a properties file, as with file system integration.

5.4.1.2 Data management with DBUnit

From a database integration point of view, requirements are twofold:

1. Put the database in a specific state during initialization
2. Assert the database is in an expected state at the end of the test

For example, for testing the whole order process, initialization has to put customers and products in setup, and after it has run, we check a new order line has been written in the database.

[DBUnit (http://www.dbunit.org/)] is a Java framework that dates back to 2002, has seen no code-related activity since January 2013 and is based on JUnit v3.x. However, it is the only one of its kind and offers both the features required above.

Creating datasets

In DBUnit, datasets can be either created "by hand" or exported from an existing database; they both mimic the database structure. They are available in two different XML file formats, standard and flat.

Code 5.5 - Standard file format sample

```
1   <?xml version="1.0" encoding="UTF-8"?>
2   <dataset>
3     <table name="TABLE_1">
4       <column>COL_0<column>
5       <column>COL_1<column>
6       <column>COL_2<column>
7       <row>
8         <value>a</value>
9         <value>b</value>
10        <value>c</value>
11      </row>
12    </table>
13    <table name="TABLE_2">
14      <column>COL_A<column>
15      <column>COL_B<column>
16      <row>
17        <value>d</value>
18        <value>e</value>
19      </row>
20      <row>
21        <value>f</value>
22        <null />
23      </row>
24    </table>
25  </dataset>
```

Code 5.6 - Flat file format sample

```
1   <?xml version="1.0" encoding="UTF-8"?>
2   <dataset>
3     <TABLE_1 COL_0="a" COL_1="b" COL_2="c" />
4     <TABLE_2 COL_A="d" COL_B="e" />
5     <TABLE_2 COL_A="f" />
6   </dataset>
```

As can be seen, standard format is much more verbose but its Document Type Definition grammar is the same across all databases:

Code 5.7 - Standard file format DTD

```
1   <!ELEMENT dataset (table+) | ANY>
2   <!ELEMENT table (column*, row*)>
3   <!ATTLIST table name CDATA #REQUIRED>
4   <!ELEMENT column (#PCDATA)>
5   <!ELEMENT row (value | null | none)*>
6   <!ELEMENT value (#PCDATA)>
7   <!ELEMENT null EMPTY>
```

On one hand, this makes it reusable from test suite to test suite; on the other hand, this also makes it almost useless, as it will not catch any table or attribute mistyping in the XML. To do that, it is necessary to use flat files **and** create the DTD. If by chance the database schema already exists, this snippet (http://www.dbunit.org/faq.html#generatedtd) connects to the database, reads the schema and writes it in a DTD file. It can then simply be referenced by the XML.

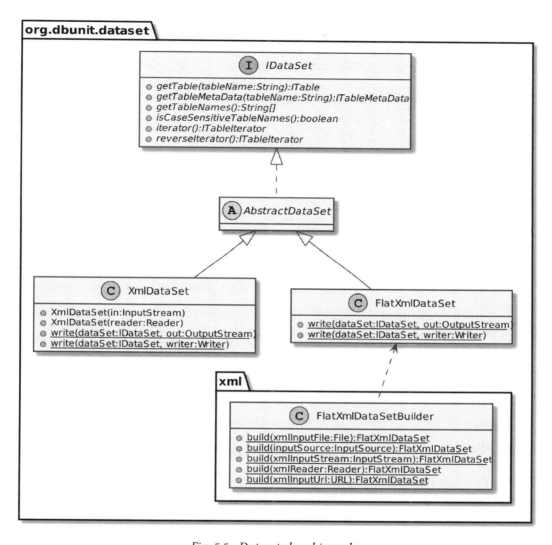

Fig. 5.5 - Dataset class hierarchy

 # Flat or standard format?

Flat format should be preferred over standard format as it is more concise and easier to write. However, if the schema seldom changes, it is better to create a DTD; if changes are more frequent, a DTD will usually bring more pain than it's worth.

Whether using standard or flat XML files, exporting a sample dataset from an existing database can be achieved with the following snippet: http://www.dbunit.org/faq.html#extract. In essence, it shows how to connect to the database, execute a query and write results and dependent the results in an XML file.

Keep datasets small and dedicated

Not only are datasets a bore to create, they become complex to handle when they grow in size, for various reasons: not NULL columns, insertion order with foreign key constraints, etc. Therefore, it is well advised to have small dedicated datasets for each testing use-case to let you better manage them. Naming of the dataset should be done in accordance with the class name.

```
public class ThisIsAnExampleTest {

    @Before
    protected void setUp() throws Exception {
        IDataSet dataset = new FlatXmlDataSetBuilder()
            .build(new File("thisIsAnExampleTest.xml"));
        // Do something with dataset
    }
}
```

Inserting datasets

Handling of datasets requires a DBUnit DatabaseOperation instance. The DatabaseOperation interface has a single method execute(IDatabaseConnection, IDataSet). Implementations of those are found as constants of the same class. Among them, some are of particular interest:

- DELETE deletes the dataset (and only the dataset) from the database
- DELETE_ALL deletes all data from the database, but **only from tables referenced in the dataset**
- INSERT inserts the dataset into the database
- CLEAN_INSERT is an ordered composite operation of DELETE_ALL then INSERT

Given that test data should be kept after test execution, it is advised to use only CLEAN_INSERT. This way, data put in reference tables (such as zip codes, countries, etc.) will not be erased.

 # True clean inserts

By using CLEAN_INSERT, only data from tables referenced in the dataset will be removed. However, some tests may create data in other tables, and this will not be removed. If they are to be tested, it may cause problems in assertions. Thus, it might be worthwhile to create a custom DatabaseOperation implementation that drops data from **all relevant** tables (of course, reference tables are excluded).

Code 5.8 - True clean inserts possible implementation

```
1   import org.dbunit.DatabaseUnitException;
2   import org.dbunit.database.IDatabaseConnection;
3   import org.dbunit.dataset.IDataSet;
4   import org.dbunit.operation.DatabaseOperation;
5
6   import java.sql.*;
7
8   public class TrueDeleteAllOperation extends DatabaseOperation {
9
10      @Override
11      public void execute(IDatabaseConnection iconn, IDataSet dataSet)
12          throws DatabaseUnitException, SQLException {
13          StringBuffer sql = new StringBuffer("DELETE FROM X; ");
14          sql.append("DELETE FROM Y; ");
15          sql.append("DELETE FROM Z; ");
16          // Append other tables if necessary
17          Connection connection = iconn.getConnection();
18          PreparedStatement statement =
19              connection.prepareStatement(sql.toString());
20          statement.executeBatch();
21      }
22  }
```

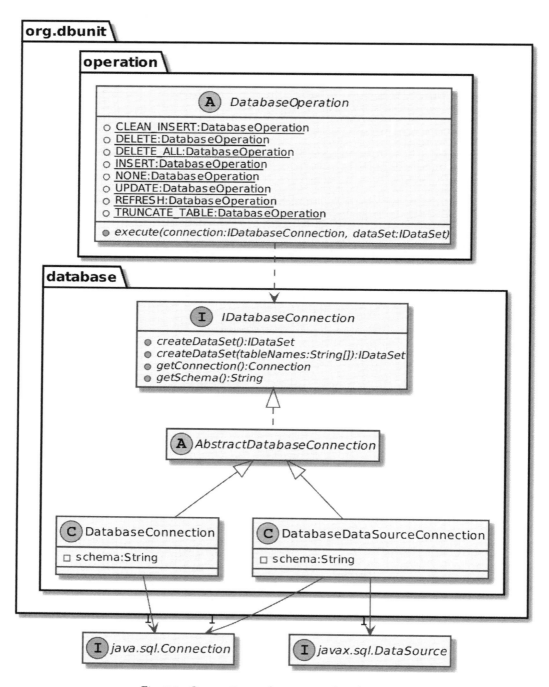

Fig. 5.6 - Connection and operation class hierarchy

Asserting datasets

Finally, when a test has run its course, the database has to be in the expected state. Doing that manually would require connecting to the database, querying tables and checking data line by line.

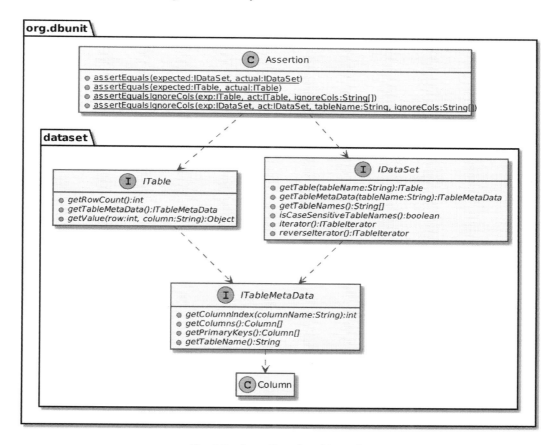

Fig. 5.7 - Assertion class hierarchy

DBUnit is able to handle all of that for us by:

1. Caching the connection in the `IConnection` implementation
2. Creating the dataset from the connection through the `createDataSet()` method
3. Providing an `Assertion` class that can compare both dataset and table contents.

Imagine a full-fledged example to test the former OrderService. This would require setting up reference customers and products, passing the order, then checking there is another new order. Let's use H2 as a persistent database (file-based) as it shows more complex setup logic.

Code 5.9.1 - DBUnit comprehensive sample code

```
1   public class OrderServiceIT {
2
3       private OrderService service;
4       private IDatabaseConnection connection;
5
6       @BeforeClass
7       protected void setUpBeforeClass() throws Exception {
8           Class.forName("org.h2.Driver");
9           Path dbPath = FileSystems.getDefault().getPath("target",
10                  "chapter5.h2.db");
11          Files.deleteIfExists(dbPath);
12          Connection connection =
13                  DriverManager.getConnection("jdbc:h2:file:target/chapter6");
14          this.connection = new DatabaseConnection(connection);
15          DatabaseConfig cfg = this.connection.getConfig();
16          cfg.setProperty(PROPERTY_DATATYPE_FACTORY, new H2DataTypeFactory());
17          Statement statement = connection.createStatement();
18          statement.addBatch("CREATE TABLE PRODUCT(ID BIGINT PRIMARY KEY)");
19          statement.addBatch("CREATE TABLE CUSTOMER(ID BIGINT PRIMARY KEY)");
20          statement.addBatch("CREATE TABLE ORDERS (" +
21                  "CUSTOMER_ID BIGINT NOT NULL, " +
22                  "PRODUCT_ID BIGINT NOT NULL, " +
23                  "PRIMARY KEY (CUSTOMER_ID, PRODUCT_ID))");
24          statement.executeBatch();
25          statement.close();
26      }
```

This part displays the setup done once before all the tests in this class. The steps are the following:

Line 8

As for any standard direct database connection, the H2 driver is loaded in memory, so JDBC knows which driver to use in order to communicate with H2 databases.

Lines 9-11

Existing database files are removed so test(s) can run from a clean state.

Line 12-13

The JDBC connection to the database is created.

Line 14

The JDBC connection is wrapped in a DBUnit connection wrapper and the latter stored as an attribute for future use.

Lines 15-16

DBUnit's default compatibility is with Apache Derby. DBUnit is explicitly configured to use H2 in order to prevent potential data type mismatch(es) between Derby and H2. Other data type factories for major database vendors are available in the library (see all packages (http://dbunit.sourceforge.net/apidocs/) starting with `org.dbunit.ext`).

Lines 17-25

Database tables used in the tests are (finally) created. This is done through standard SQL DDL statements.

Code 5.9.2 - DBUnit comprehensive sample code

```
1    @AfterClass
2    protected void tearDownAfterClass() throws Exception {
3        connection.close();
4    }
```

It is a good practice to close the connection to the database after the tests have completed.

In-memory databases are only accessible during a JVM run. In a test context, this means this step could well be omitted with no side-effects. However, closing the connection should be a habit and makes the above snippet a template reusable in other scenarios.

Code 5.9.3 - DBUnit comprehensive sample code

```
1    @BeforeMethod
2    protected void setUp() throws Exception {
3        Connection connection = this.connection.getConnection();
4        CustomerRepository customerRepository =
5                new CustomerRepository(connection);
6        ProductRepository prdRepository = new ProductRepository(connection);
7        OrderRepository orderRepository = new OrderRepository(connection);
8        service = new OrderService(
9                customerRepository, orderRepository, prdRepository);
10   }
```

As in previous tests, before each test case, the setup initializes the instance under test so as to have no side-effect from state changed in previous test cases.

Code 5.9.4 - DBUnit comprehensive sample code

```
1    @Test
2    public void order_should_save_order_with_product_and_customer()
3            throws Exception {
4        FlatXmlDataSetBuilder builder = new FlatXmlDataSetBuilder();
5        Path initPath = FileSystems.getDefault().getPath("target",
6                "test-classes", "chapter5", "OrderServiceText-init.xml");
7        IDataSet dataSet = builder.build(initPath.toFile());
8        CLEAN_INSERT.execute(this.connection, dataSet);
9        service.order(2L, 2L);
10       Path expectedPath = FileSystems.getDefault().getPath("target",
11               "test-classes", "chapter5", "OrderServiceText-expected.xml");
12       IDataSet expected = builder.build(expectedPath.toFile());
13       IDataSet actual = connection.createDataSet(new String[]{"ORDERS"});
14       assertEquals(expected, actual);
```

```
15        }
16    }
```

The test itself does the following:

Line 4-8:
>The database is set in the expected state. In this case, an existing file is loaded to populate the database. Since there are no other test cases, this could also have been done during setup. Also, it would have been enough to use INSERT instead of CLEAN_INSERT. However, as for closing the database connection, it makes sense to support more advanced usages, such as having multiple test cases (a likely occurrence in real-life projects).

Line 9:
>The method to be tested (at last!)

Line 10-14:
>An expected data set is created from a provided file. Then the actual data is read from the database and compared. If both are equal, the test passes; if not, it fails.

 Evaluate ROI carefully
>This example demonstrates that integration testing Return Over Investment should carefully be evaluated as the setup code is quite long and error prone compared to the feature under test. Trivial data access code should probably not be tested.

5.4.1.3 Setting up data with DBSetup

Using DBUnit to set up data at test initialization requires tons of XML which is:

Time-consuming
>DBUnit XML files mimic the database tables structure. Columns are repeated

as XML attributes on each line, so that writing an XML file involves copy-pasting and changing the value.

Also, XML is declarative only and prevents tests and loops.

Error-prone

XML is not compiled. At best, it can be validated against a Document Type Definition (or an XML schema). Anyone who has ever generated a DTD (http://dbunit.sourceforge.net/faq.html#generatedtd) for DBUnit knows the configuration to use in both tests and IDE with no error takes time.

DBSetup (http://dbsetup.ninja-squad.com/) is an initiative aimed at correcting those drawbacks for inserting data. However, it does not provide ways to validate data after test execution.

5.4.2 NoSQL Database integration

While Integration Testing benefits from SQL standards, NoSQL offers no such standardization: each product might have an associated product dedicated to help with Integration Testing… or not. At the time of this writing, only MongoDB (https://www.mongodb.org/) offers such a testing framework.

5.4.2.1 MongoDB integration

MongoDB is a NoSQL document database. From a developer point of view, once MongoDB has been installed on a server, using this particular database instance looks as follows:

```
MongoClient client = new MongoClient("localhost", 27017);
DB main = mongoClient.getDB("main");
// Now use main to get collections and stuff
```

This snippet assumes a MongoDB instance is running on localhost and listening on port 27017. For testing purposes, this means one has:

- To make sure the MongoDB binaries are available on the system

- If not, download and extract them
- To have permissions to setup MongoDB
- To get it up and running during test startup
- To shut it down during cleanup

It is possible, but not exactly worthwile from a ROI perspective. This process can however be replaced by using Fongo (https://github.com/fakemongo/fongo).

> Fongo is an in-memory java implementation of Mongo. It intercepts calls to the standard mongo-java-driver for finds, updates, inserts, removes and other methods. The primary use is for lightweight unit testing where you don't want to spin up a Mongo process.

 ## Missing features and limitations

Not all MongoDB features are included in Fongo and in some cases, the ones that are included might be limited, so caution is advised. As Fongo and MongoDB are changing on a very rapid basis, it is advised to check the gaps before relying on Fongo.

Fongo usage is very straightforward: it provides a `Fongo` class that offers more or less the same methods as the standard `MongoClient` but the former does not share any contract with the latter. However, Fongo also provides a `MockMongoClient` that both inherits from `MongoClient` and wraps a `Fongo` instance.

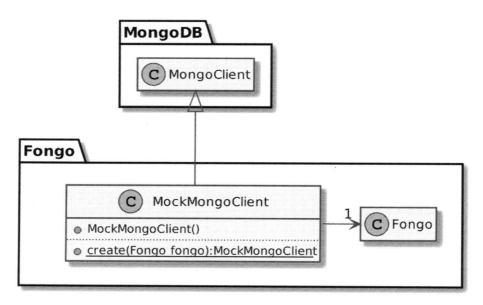

Fig. 5.8 - Fongo core classes

That requires application design to allow for the Mongo client to be injected. The starting point would look something like the following:

Code 5.10 - MongoDB starting design

```
1   import com.mongodb.*;
2
3   import java.net.UnknownHostException;
4   import java.util.*;
5
6   public class MongoDbRepositoryNaiveSample {
7
8       private DB database;
9
10      public MongoDbRepositoryNaiveSample(String host, int port)
11              throws UnknownHostException {
12          MongoClient client = new MongoClient(host, port);
13          database = client.getDB("customerDb");
14      }
15
```

```
16      public List<Customer> getAllCustomers() {
17          DBCollection collection = database.getCollection("customer");
18          DBCursor cursor = collection.find();
19          List<Customer> customers = new ArrayList<>();
20
21          try {
22              while (cursor.hasNext()) {
23                  DBObject object = cursor.next();
24                  Integer id = (Integer) object.get("_id");
25                  Customer customer = new Customer();
26                  customer.setId((long) id);
27                  customers.add(customer);
28              }
29          } finally {
30              cursor.close();
31          }
32
33          return customers;
34      }
35 }
```

Updating the design would involve replacing the above constructor code with this:

Code 5.11 - MongoDB testable design

```
1      private DB database;
2
3      public MongoDbRepositoryTestableSample(MongoClient client) {
4          database = client.getDB("customerDb");
5      }
6      . . .
7 }
```

Nothing fancy here: simply that the lessons for achieving a testing-friendly design from *Chapter 3 - Test-Friendly Design* have been applied. At this point, testing becomes very easy:

Code 5.12 - MongoDB test

```
1    import com.github.fakemongo.Fongo;
2    import com.mongodb.*;
3    import org.testng.annotations.*;
4
5    import java.net.UnknownHostException;
6    import java.util.List;
7
8    import static com.mongodb.WriteConcern.ACKNOWLEDGED;
9    import static org.testng.Assert.*;
10
11   public class MongoDbRepositoryIT {
12
13       private MongoDbRepositoryTestableSample repository;
14
15       private MockMongoClient client;
16
17       @BeforeTest
18       protected void setUp() throws UnknownHostException {
19           Fongo fongo = new Fongo("main");
20           client = MockMongoClient.create(fongo);
21           repository = new MongoDbRepositoryTestableSample(client);
22       }
23
24       @Test
25       public void should_return_all_customers() {
26           DB database = client.getDB("customerDb");
27           DBCollection collection = database.getCollection("customer");
28           for (int i = 0; i < 5; i++) {
29               collection.insert(ACKNOWLEDGED, new BasicDBObject("_id", i));
30           }
31
32           List<Customer> customer = repository.getAllCustomers();
33           assertNotNull(customer);
34           assertEquals(customer.size(), 5);
35       }
36   }
```

Here is the explanation of the code.

Line 19

> A new `Fongo` instance is created. Notice the constructor requires a `String` parameter: it is the instance's name but plays no role whatsoever.

Line 20

> Create the Mongo client required for the class under test at line 24, using the `MockMongoClient.create()` factory method.

Lines 26-30

> Set up the database state by adding a new `DBObject` to the Mongo collection.

5.5 eMail integration

Many applications have email-sending capabilities, while some have email-receiving ones. This is generally achieved by connecting to a Simple Mail Transfer Protocol server (respectively POP3/IMAP) and issuing the relevant commands.

A huge Integration Testing issue occurs when application use-cases require to send or receive emails. As with databases, the components responsible for those features can be mocked, but this does not guarantee that they will work correctly.

Fortunately, two fake SMTP servers are available for use during tests:

- Dumbster (http://quintanasoft.com/dumbster/) is a fake SMTP server, where outbound mails are stored for later retrieval and asserts
- Greenmail (http://www.icegreen.com/greenmail/) is an SMTP, POP3 and IMAP server with SSL support all rolled into one

Greenmail has two big advantages over Dumbster: it is feature-complete regarding emails and is available as a Maven dependency (refer to *Chapter 4 - Automated testing* for a refresher if needed) on repo1.

Greenmail main classes are:

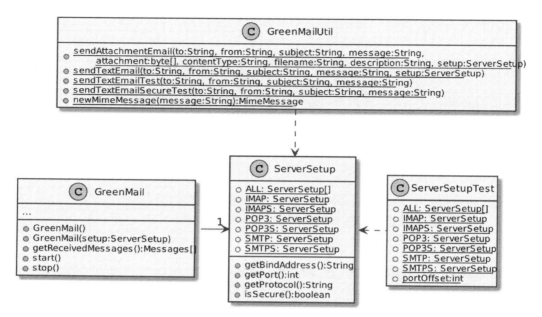

Fig. 5.9 - Green mail core classes

ⓘ Greenmail is Grails favorite

Greenmail is also available as a plugin for the Grails platform.

The Greenmail root class is `GreenMail` which represents the email server itself. It can respectively be started and stopped with its `start()` and `stop()` methods.

Port numbers restriction

On *nix systems, launching processes that bind ports below number 1024 requires root privileges. Calling `start()` with no arguments calls `start(ServerSetup.ALL)`, using default ports (*e.g.* 25 for SMTP, 11P for POP3, etc.) that are below this limit. In order to be portable across all Operating Systems, one should call `start(ServerSetupTest.ALL)` instead, that set all default protocol ports to their default value **plus** the `ServerSetupTest.offset` value (which is settable).

1. To get the messages received by the GreenMail fake server, call the receiveMessages() method on the GreenMail instance

Code 5.13 - Receiving messages with Greenmail

```java
@BeforeClass
protected void setUpBeforeClass() {
        greenMail = new GreenMail();
        greenMail.start();
}


@AfterClass
protected void tearDownAfterClass() {
        greenMail.stop();
}


@Test
public void send_should_send_mail_message() throws Exception {
        sender.send("Hello world!", "This is a dummy message",
                "from@dummy.com", "to@dummy.com");
        Message[] messages = greenMail.getReceivedMessages();

        assertNotNull(messages);
        assertEquals(messages.length, 1);

        Message message = messages[0];
        Address[] froms = message.getFrom();

        assertNotNull(froms);
        assertEquals(froms.length, 1);
        assertMessageEquals(froms[0], "from@dummy.com");
}
```

The previous code gets the messages from the fake server, checks the number of received messages, get the single message and then checks the sender. Other data could also be checked (sender, subject, body).

2. To send messages to the Greenmail fake server, call the static GreenMailUtil.sendTextEmailTest() method (or its secured protocol ports

counterpart `GreenMailUtil.sendTextEmailSecureTest()` instead)

Code 5.14 - Sending messages with Greenmail

```
@BeforeClass
protected void setUpBeforeClass() {
        greenMail = new GreenMail();
        greenMail.setUser("test", "test");
        greenMail.start();
}


@AfterClass
protected void tearDownAfterClass() {
        greenMail.stop();
}


@Test
public void receive_should_receive_all_mail_messages() throws Exception {
        GreenMailUtil.sendTextEmailTest("to@dummy.com", "from@dummy1.com",
                "Hello world!", "This is a dummy message");
        GreenMailUtil.sendTextEmailTest("to@dummy.com", "from@dummy2.com",
                "Hello world!", "This is another dummy message");
        Message[] messages = receiver.receive("test", "test");

        assertNotNull(messages);
        assertEquals(messages.length, 2);
}
```

The above code uses Greenmail to send two dummy email messages.

⚷ Reuse the Fake throughout your tests

As for other infrastructure resource Fakes, it is advised to keep the Fake instance up throughout the test suite for even Fakes have startup cost. TestNG is definitely your friend here as the Fake can be started in any of the lifecycle hooks depending on the context.

5.6 FTP integration

Some applications require interacting with an FTP server, either uploading or downloading files. As for other components interacting with infrastructure resources, FTP-responsible components have to be tested by using the techniques already seen above.

In this area, the MockFTPServer (http://mockftpserver.sourceforge.net/) project is a great library that offers two different capabilities depending on the entry-point class used:

1. `org.mockftpserver.fake.FakeFtpServer` represents a fake FTP server
2. `org.mockftpserver.stub.StubFtpServer` is an abstraction over an FTP server that can be stubbed with behavior required for testing

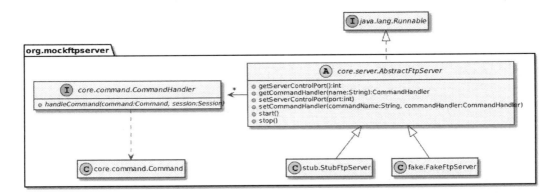

Fig. 5.10 - MockFTPServer root classes

As with the Greenmail server, the server's lifecyle can be managed through the `start()` and `stop()` methods.

 Port numbers restriction

By default, the server will attempt to bind to port 21 (FTP's default port). As it requires root privileges on *nix systems, it is more than recommended to call the `setServerControlPort()` method with a port number higher than 1024 before starting it.

5.6.1 Fake FTP server

FakeFtpServer is one of the two components of MockFTPServer: the Fake server is set a virtual filesystem, complete with accounts and permissions.

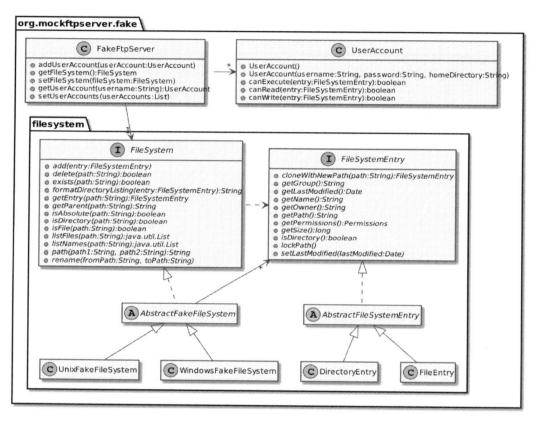

Fig. 5.11 - Fake FTP server class hierarchy

When the server is issued FTP commands, it is the filesystem that is used. The API offers two concrete filesystem implementations, one *nix-like and one Windows-like. The good thing is that since the filesystem is virtual, either of the two implementations can be plugged-in **regardless** of the physical Operating System that the tests are executed on, meaning one should target the production filesystem.

As an example, imagine a component that gets text files from FTP servers and that needs to be tested. Here is some sample code to achieve that, using the Fake server:

Code 5.15 - Setting up a Fake FTP server

```
1   @BeforeClass
2   protected void setUpBeforeClass() {
3       client = new FtpGetComponent("localhost", 2021, "test", "test");
4           fs = new UnixFakeFileSystem();
5       server = new FakeFtpServer();
6       server.setServerControlPort(2021);
7       server.setFileSystem(fs);
8       server.addUserAccount(new UserAccount("test", "test", "/"));
9       server.start();
10  }
11
12  @AfterClass
13  protected void tearDownAfterClass() {
14          server.stop();
15  }
16
17  @Test
18  public void get_file_should_contain_hello_world() throws IOException {
19          String tmpDir = System.getProperty("java.io.tmpdir");
20          Path path = Paths.get(tmpDir, "dummy.txt");
21          Files.deleteIfExists(path);
22          fs.add(new FileEntry("/dummy.txt", "Hello world!"));
23          client.getTextFile(path.toString(), "/dummy.txt");
24          assertTrue(Files.exists(path));
25          List<String> lines = Files.readAllLines(path);
26          assertNotNull(lines);
27          assertFalse(lines.isEmpty());
28          assertEquals(lines.size(), 1);
29          String line = lines.iterator().next();
30          assertEquals(line, "Hello world!");
31  }
```

The Fake server is good enough for typical FTP server behavior. However, it cannot simulate error behavior. For this, custom-made stubs are required.

5.6.2 Stub FTP server

In order to provide the desired behavior during test execution, it is possible to provide custom CommandHandlers that are invoked when calling a specific FTP command.

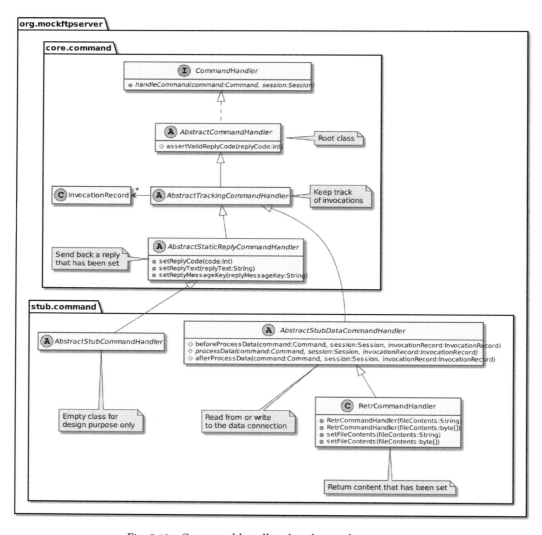

Fig. 5.12 - Command handler class hierarchy overview

In this context, FTP commands are not those that are typed by users on the command line (ls, cd, etc.) but those of the FTP **protocol** http://en. wikipedia.org/wiki/List_of_FTP_commands.

MockFTPServer provides a default command handler implementation for each FTP command, and there are many. Note that command handler classes are also used internally in the Fake server. The following diagram displays the upper levels of the CommandHandler class hierarchy.

In regard to the previous example, instead of using a Fake server with a file added at the root, one could provide a command handler that returns the file on RETR commands. Line 28 from the previous code can be replaced with the following:

Code 5.16 - Using the RETR default command handler

```
46    (RetrCommandHandler) server.getCommandHandler(RETR);
47  handler.setFileContents("Hello world!");
48        client.getTextFile(path.toString(), "/dummy.txt");
49        assertTrue(Files.exists(path));
```

Notes:

1. The Stub server does not allow a filesystem to be set.
2. A more advanced (and expensive) setup would be to extend RetrCommandHandler and override processData() to analyze the parameters of the Command argument. If it is "/dummy.txt" then return the content, otherwise send the appropriate reply (500).

Code 5.17 - A custom command handler

```java
import org.mockftpserver.core.command.*;
import org.mockftpserver.core.session.Session;
import org.mockftpserver.stub.command.RetrCommandHandler;

import static org.mockftpserver.core.command.ReplyCodes.READ_FILE_ERROR;

public class AdvancedRetrCommandHandler extends RetrCommandHandler {

    private byte[] fileContents = new byte[0];

    public AdvancedRetrCommandHandler() {}

    public AdvancedRetrCommandHandler(String fileContents) {
        setFileContents(fileContents);
    }

    public AdvancedRetrCommandHandler(byte[] fileContents) {
        setFileContents(fileContents);
    }

    @Override
    protected void processData(Command command,
        Session session, InvocationRecord invocationRecord) {
        String arg = command.getParameter(0);
        if ("/dummy.txt".equals(arg)) {
            super.processData(command, session, invocationRecord);
        } else {
          sendReply(session, READ_FILE_ERROR, null, null, new Object[]{arg});
        }
    }

    @Override
    public void setFileContents(byte[] fileContents) {
        super.setFileContents(fileContents);
        this.fileContents = fileContents;
    }
}
```

37 }
_____

At this point, using the handler is a simple as calling `server.set(RETR,  new AdvancedRetrCommandHandler())`.

 Stub or Fake FTP server?

Having more than one option always forces one to make a choice. In most contexts, it is better to use the Fake server as it a) requires less effort and b) makes code more readable. It is recommended to use the Stub server only if the testing requirements go beyond the Fake's features.

5.7 Summary

This chapter detailed how to test integration with some important infrastructure resources, such as filesystems, system time, databases, email servers and FTP servers, as well as tools that help in doing so.

There is no common lesson here, just to be aware of the Faking tool appropriate for each resource. However, in this day and age, most resources that need integrating with are web services. Those will be covered in the next chapter.

6. Testing Integration with Web Services

This chapter presents tools and techniques to test integration with specific infrastructure resources, web services. Web services are ubitiquous nowadays, and nearly every software consumes (or produces) one or more web services in a way or another.

Commons web service use-cases include:

- Authentication with OAuth2, from a variety of providers
- Cloud Infrastructure Management with Amazon Web Services and others
- Printing
- And last but not least, Data Providers

From a tecnical point of view, web services fall into one of two broad technologies, SOAP or REST. Each will have its own section.

6.1 REST Web Services

REST is often described in the litterature as an architectural style. However, its implementations in the real-world might not be a pure as it is intended. In essence, calling a REST web service should be dependent on only two factors: a) the HTTP verb (GET, POST, etc.) and b) the URL.

In all cases, requirements for the testing Fake implementation include the following:

1. Easy to set up
2. Easy to read, thus to maintain
3. No need for an application server, as the tested SUT might not be a webapp
4. Also address corner-cases around REST such as cookies and URL parameters

6.1.1 Spark to the rescue

Fortunately, there exists in the Java ecosystem a library matching all those requirements named Spark (http://www.sparkjava.com/). Spark is a so-called *micro-
web-framework* and offers an embedded web server, that makes it completely
independent and a perfect match for integration testing.

Here is a general overview of the Spark API:

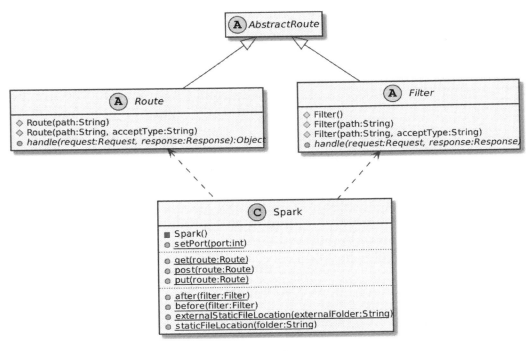

Fig. 6.1 - Spark overview

Spark's embedded server default port is 4067. This can be overriden by calling Spark.setPort() with the desired port as a parameter.

Basically, the Spark class is at the API core. One can add Routes to it, mapped to a given HTTP method. When the embedded Spark server is browsed through the relevant HTTP method, the route's handle() method is called. Filters are very similar to routes, but plays the same role as Servlet Filters as routes for Servlets.

Here is a very basic example:

Code 6.1 - Basic Spark example

```
1  get(new Route("/hello/world") {
2      @Override
3      public Object handle(Request request, Response response) {
4          return "Hello world!";
5      }
6  });
```

Given the previous code, any GET request for /hello/world will print Hello world! in the response stream.

 ## Starting Spark

Calling any of Spark's HTTP verb methods will also start the server.

6.1.2 Practical how-to

REST web services usually return one of the following along with an HTTP return code:

1. An XML response
2. A JSON response
3. Nothing

Let us see how Spark can be leveraged to do this. The two first cases are similar, a complex response needs to be returned. There are several ways to achieve this, let's go through each of them, taking a simple JSON response as an example.

1. The fastest and less expensive way is to directly write the required response as the return value, not forgetting to set the correct MIME type beforehand through Response's type() method.

Code 6.2 - Simple JSON route

```
1   public Object handle(Request request, Response response) {
2       response.type("application/json");
3       return "{ \"hello\" : \"world!\" }";
4   }
```

2. Alternatively, and for more complex response types, it is possible to get a reference of an external JSON file, read its content, and return it. This is not only boring, but also error-prone.

Code 6.3 - File read JSON route

```
1   @Override
2   public Object handle(Request request, Response response) {
3       InputStream in = getClass().getClassLoader()
4           .getResourceAsStream("chapter6/hello.json");
5       try (Reader reader = new InputStreamReader(in)) {
6           StringBuffer buffer = new StringBuffer();
7           int read;
8           char[] cbuf = new char[1024];
9           while ((read = reader.read(cbuf)) != -1) {
10              buffer.append(cbuf, 0, read);
11          }
12          response.type("application/json");
13          return buffer.toString();
14      } catch (IOException e) {
15          halt(500, "Could not get a hold on hello.json");
16          return null;
17      }
18  }
```

Keep the in mind the exception handling block, it will be explained shortly below.

3. The best solution is offered by Spark with the `TemplateViewRoute` class. It provides the same service as the above boilerplate code **out-of-the-box**. It has two available templating engines implementations, one based on Freemarker (http://freemarker.org/), the other on Apache Velocity (http://velocity.apache.org/).

Here are core classes used by template routes:

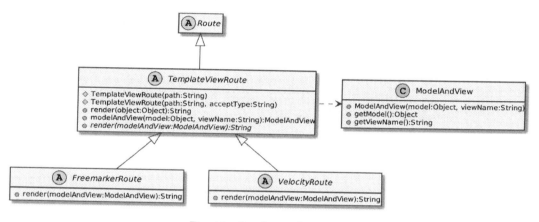

Fig. 6.2 - Spark template routes

Code 6.4 - Template JSON route

```
1   @Override
2   public Object handle(Request request, Response response) {
3       response.type("application/json");
4       Map<String, String> model = new HashMap<>();
5       // Add any required data to the model
6       String view = "chapter6/hello.json";
7       return modelAndView(model, view);
8   }
```

The following code produces exactly the same output as the previous one.

Dynamic templating and maintainability

The returned content can also be dynamic, thanks to any of the two templating engines power. In order to go this way, just fill the model HashMap and the templating engine will replace keys found in the template with the relevant values. Loops and conditions are also possible: just browse the documentation. All these features can feel quite empowering. However, keep in mind that implementing logic and such is by far the quickest way to make tests complex, so less readable, thus more expensive to maintain...

Spring Framework alternative

If the Faked REST resource is available and uses of the Spring Framework, consider the usage of MockRestServiceServer (http://docs.spring.io/spring/docs/current/javadoc-api/org/springframework/test/web/client/MockRestServiceServer.html)

6.1.2.1 Halt

Halting deserves a special mention: it stops the current request within the route. It can be invoked with no argument, the status code, the body or both. The entry point to halt methods is the AbstractRoute class. Underneath, they will throw HaltException.

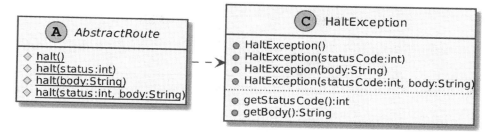

Fig. 6.3 - Spark halt

6.1.3 Github comprehensive example

Github is a good data web service provider and has dedicated API for developers. As an exercise, let's create a Fake provider for a very limited scope, *e.g.* the users list (https://api.github.com/users). Other services could likewise be Faked.

Step 1

> Browse the URL and copy paste a limited number of elements (say 2 or 3) of the returned JSON array into a users.json file.

Step 2

> Create the route to serve the users.json file.

Code 6.5 - Github users list route

```java
1   import spark.*;
2   import spark.template.velocity.VelocityRoute;
3
4   import java.util.HashMap;
5
6   public abstract class GithubUsersListRoute extends VelocityRoute {
7
8       public GithubUsersListRoute() {
9           super("/users");
10      }
11
12      @Override
```

```
13    public Object handle(Request request, Response response) {
14        response.type("application/json");
15        return modelAndView(new HashMap<String, String>(),
16            "chapter6/users.json");
17    }
18 }
```

Step 3

Bind the route to the GET HTTP method by calling get(new GithubUsersListRoute()). That's it for a Fake Github API testing server! If necessary, repeat for other required web service URLs.

 ## "Tainted" REST services

By convention, REST services should be stateless. In the real life, however, users should be able to stay logged in, requiring some form of state, generally cookies. The above section just described simple REST. If the need be, refer to the Spark documentation (http://www.sparkjava.com/readme.html), as it addresses every conceivable use-case. Some great examples include:

- https://code.google.com/p/spark-java/#Examples
- https://github.com/perwendel/spark-template-velocity/ blob/master/src/test/java/spark/template/velocity/example/ VelocityExample.java

6.2 SOAP Web Services

Compared to REST, SOAP web services (http://en.wikipedia.org/wiki/SOAP) are more heavyweight and structured. For developpers, this means getting hold of the Web Service Definition Language (http://en.wikipedia.org/wiki/Web_Services_Description_Language) (WSDL) file and generate the Java client files with the help of a dedicated framework at development time. At runtime, just calling the client entry-point class (depending on the generating framework) is enough.

SOAP Web Services development relies on the WSDL. The WSDL represents the contract, and it should be honored by any web service, Fake or otherwise.

SoapUI (http://www.soapui.org/) is **the** tool to use when developping Fake services. It offers many features, all related to Web Services:

- Inspection of existing Web Services
- Invocation of existing Web Services
- Development of new Web Services
- Faking of Web Services
- Functional, Load, Compliance and Secuirty of running Web Services

SoapUI offers many more features with its Pro flavor; however, the standard flavor is more than enough for Integration Testing. Note REST as well as SOAP Web Services are handled by SoapUI, but it is the author's opinion that it is overkill compared to Spark.

Installing the product is straightforward: download the installer related to your platform and follow instructions to install the software. The rest of this section implies SoapUI has been installed and is running.

SoapUI and REST

SoapUI version 5 also offers REST resources fakes. However, Spark is far more lightweight and easier to use. Readers wanting to use SoapUI REST testing features can read the referant online documentation (http://www.soapui.org/REST-Testing/getting-started.html).

6.2.1 SoapUI basics

As many Integrated Development Environments around, SoapUI is based on workspace, tabs and projects.

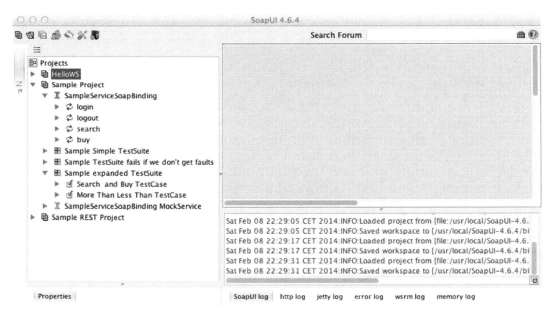

Fig. 6.4 - SoapUI IDE overview

As an example, the IP2Geo service (http://www.cdyne.com/api/ip-location/) will be used as an example; it finds the location of any IP address. It is a commercial product and requires an API key but provides a key - *for testing purposes*. Anyway, the goal is to fake the aforementioned service.

Quick preview

To get a quick overview of the IP2Geo service, open this URL in any browser: http://ws.cdyne.com/ip2geo/ip2geo.asmx/ResolveIP?ipAddress= 173.194.34.39&licenseKey=0. Two different parameters are used:

1. ipAddress is the IP address to locate
2. licenseKey is the Licence key provided by the service provider, the value is the dummy key (0) offered by SoapUI for evaluation purposes

This will return the following snippet:

Code 6.6 - IP2Geo response example

```
1    <IPInformation>
2        <City>Mountain View</City>
3        <StateProvince>CA</StateProvince>
4        <Country>United States</Country>
5        <Organization/>
6        <Latitude>37.4192</Latitude>
7        <Longitude>-122.0574</Longitude>
8        <AreaCode>0</AreaCode>
9        <TimeZone/>
10       <HasDaylightSavings>false</HasDaylightSavings>
11       <Certainty>90</Certainty>
12       <RegionName/>
13       <CountryCode>US</CountryCode>
14   </IPInformation>
```

Here is a summary of bindings specified in the WSDL:

Table 6.1 - IP2Geo bindings description

Binding	Description
IP2GeoSoap	SOAP 1.1 service version
IP2GeoSoap12	SOAP 1.2 service version
IP2GeoHttpGet	GET service flavor (as used above)
IP2GeoHttpPost	POST service flavor

Note the last two bindings are not SOAP bindings in the true sense of the term, as neither request is wrapped in a SOAP enveloppe.

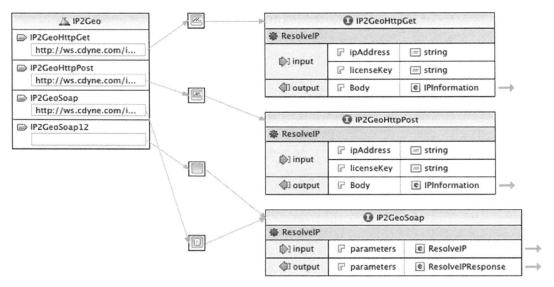

Fig. 6.5 - IP2Geo WSDL

Create a SoapUI project by selecting File | New SOAP Project. Fill in the fields in the popup as follows:

Project Name
> IP2Geo

Initial WSDL
> http://ws.cdyne.com/ip2geo/ip2geo.asmx?wsdl

Check "Store all file paths in project relative to project file" and click OK.

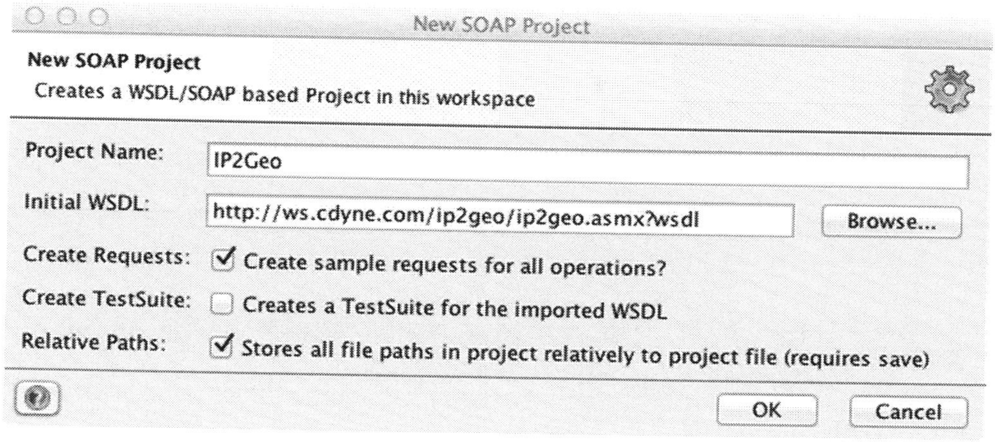

Fig. 6.6 - Creating a new project

Choose the project path and a new project should appear in the workspace, with the following structure:

Fig. 6.7 - IP2Geo project created

Right-click on the IP2GeoSoap binding (JAX-WS client tool cannot generate code for the 1.2 version), and click on "Generate Mock Service". In the opening popup, fill in the fields as follows:

Path /ip2geo/ip2geo.asmx

Port 8088 (leave default)

Generate MockService

Generate MockService
Set options for generated MockOperations for this Interface

MockService:	`<create>` ⬍
Operations:	☑ ResolveIP
	[Select all] [Unselect all]
Path:	/ip2geo/ip2geo.asmx
Port:	8088
Add Endpoint:	☑ Adds the MockServices endpoint to the mocked Interface
Start MockService:	☐ Starts the MockService immediately

[OK] [Cancel]

Fig. 6.8 - Creating a new Mock service

In the opening popup, leave the default Mock Service name and click OK. The newly created Mock Service appears in the previously created IP2Geo project.

Fig. 6.9 - The newly created Mock service

Double-click on the existing response named "Response 1", this will open it to be edited. One should update values according to one's needs.

Code 6.7 - Fake IP2Geo response example

```
1  <soap:Envelope xmlns:soap="http://www.w3.org/2003/05/soap-envelope"
2                 xmlns:ws="http://ws.cdyne.com/">
3     <soap:Header/>
4     <soap:Body>
5        <ws:ResolveIPResponse>
6           <ws:ResolveIPResult>
7              <ws:City>New York</ws:City>
8              <ws:StateProvince>NY</ws:StateProvince>
9              <ws:Country>United States</ws:Country>
10             <ws:Organization />
11             <ws:Latitude>40.689215</ws:Latitude>
12             <ws:Longitude>-74.0445419</ws:Longitude>
13             <ws:AreaCode>0</ws:AreaCode>
14             <ws:TimeZone />
15             <ws:HasDaylightSavings>false</ws:HasDaylightSavings>
16             <ws:Certainty>100</ws:Certainty>
17             <ws:RegionName />
18             <ws:CountryCode>US</ws:CountryCode>
19          </ws:ResolveIPResult>
20       </ws:ResolveIPResponse>
21    </soap:Body>
22  </soap:Envelope>
```

The final step is to start a SoapUI server that returns the Fake response. Right-click on the Mock Service and select "Start". The SoapUI log should display something like this:

```
1  ...:INFO:Mounted WSDL for interface [IP2GeoSoap12]
2           at [/ip2geo/ip2geo.asmx?WSDL]
3  ...:INFO:Started mockService [IP2GeoSoap12 MockService]
4           on port [8088] at path [/ip2geo/ip2geo.asmx]
```

At this point, any **SOAP** request (this excludes just typing the URL in the browser) to the endpoint http://localhost:8088/ip2geo/ip2geo.asmx will return the Fake response crafted above. It is easy to test the running mock service. Just double-click the corresponding request to open the popup, the left panel should display the SOAP request. Then :

- Set the URL to the previously configured URL http://localhost:8088/ip2geo/ip2geo.asmx
- Submit the request by clicking the Submit button (the arrow located in the popup window upper left corner)

The Fake response should appear in the right panel:

Fig. 6.10 - Submitting a request to get the Mock response

6.2.2 Using SoapUI programmatically

Using SoapUI programmatically means using Fake services outside SoapUI IDE and inside automated tests. It only requires:

1. Setting the SoapUI library on the classpath (as well as other required libraries)
2. Getting a hold on the previously created project XML

SoapUI API is quite big; fortunately, only a very limited subset is necessary for our purpose.

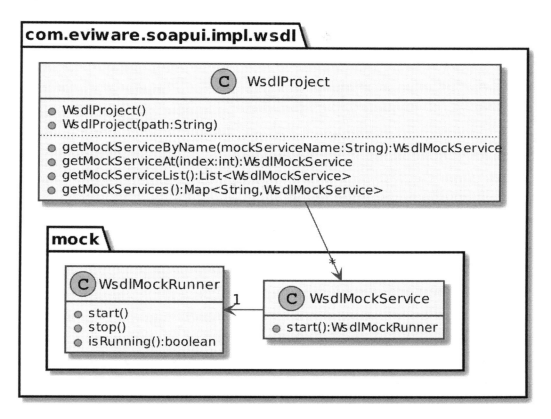

Fig. 6.11 - SoapUI API minimal extract

WsdlProject

> WsdlProject represents the project created with SoapUI IDE, including the entire list of Mock Services. WsdlProject offers methods to get references on those Mock Services, either individually or as collections.

WsdlMockService

> WsdlMockService represents a single Fake Service in the SoapUI project. It can be started: SoapUI will create a SOAP server that will return the Fake Response associated with the service.

WsdlMockRunner

WsdlMockRunner is the way to manage the lifecycle of a Mock Service.

Here is an snippet showing how to set up the previous SoapUI Mock Service in a TestNG test:

Code 6.8 - Setting up a SoapUI Mock Service

```
1  @BeforeClass
2  protected void setUpBeforeClass() throws Exception {
3      WsdlProject project = new WsdlProject(
4          "src/test/resources/chapter7/IP2Geo-soapui-project.xml");
5      WsdlMockService fakeService =
6          project.getMockServiceByName("MockService 1");
7      runner = fakeService.start();
8  }
```

The corresponding clean up code is the following:

Code 6.9 - Properly shutting down the Mock Service

```
1      if (runner != null & runner.isRunning()) {
2          runner.stop();
3      }
4  }
5  }
```

6.2.3 Dynamic response handling

There are 3 different ways to return dynamic responses:

1. Either provide multiple responses and dispatch one of them based on some parameter
2. Or provide a parameterized response
3. Or a combination of the two above

Beware of complex logic in test cases

It is advised to design and return a single static Fake Response for each test case, as dynamic behavior in tests decreases maintainability while increasing the risk of bugs. However, depending on each specific context, dynamic responses might sometimes be a viable option.

6.2.3.1 Dispatch between multiple responses

In order to enable response dispatch, double-click the desired operation - it opens a window with all defined responses, then add new responses. There are several dispatch options listed in the list-box:

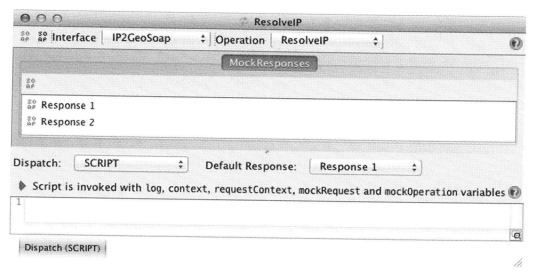

Fig. 6.12 - SoapUI dynamic responses

 # Multiple responses default behavior

Script (see below) is the default dispatch method, but the script itself is blank if not set. Thus, if multiple Fake responses have been defined for a single Mock Service, the one set as default response, which is the first created, will be returned.

Sequence

With sequence dispatch, the first call returns the first response, the second call returns the second response and so on. After the last response has been returned, it cycles back to the first.

 This behavior means that if only a single Fake Response has been specified, it will be returned on every subsequent calls.

Random

As its name implies, random dispatch returns a response at random amongst those defined.

 In regard to Integration Testing, randomness is far from being an interesting property and thus Random a rarely used dispatch method (if at all).

XPath

XPath dispatch returns responses according to XPath expressions matching (or not) the request content. Those expressions are evaluated sequentially; the first match will return the associated response. If none matches, the specified default response will be returned.

As an example, let us define a simple XPath match that checks the requested IP address and return the response named whose name matches the expression value.

```
declare namespace ws='http://ws.cdyne.com/';
//ws:ResolveIP/ws:ipAddress
```

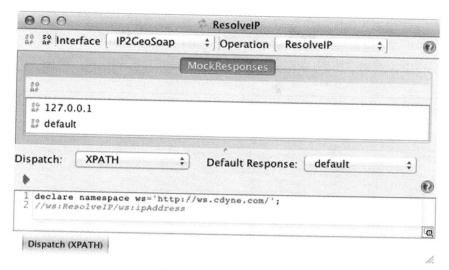

Fig. 6.13 - XPath match

Thus, an `ipAdress` value of `127.0.0.1` will return the similarly named response, while other values will return the `default` one.

Query Match

As for XPath dispatch above, Query Match dispatch evaluates XPath expresions. However, when XPath directly binds XPath values to response names, Query Match adds an indirection level that requires configuration.

As an example, let us define a simple Query Match mapping the following algorithm:

```
IF
    requested IP address == 127.0.0.1
THEN
    return "New York"
ELSE
    return "Washington"
```

In order to achieve that, the following configuration is required:

- XPath rule:

```
declare namespace ws='http://ws.cdyne.com/';
//ws:ResolveIP/ws:ipAddress
```

- Expected Value: 127.0.0.1
- Dispatch To: New York
- Default Response: Washington

The complete configuration renders to the following:

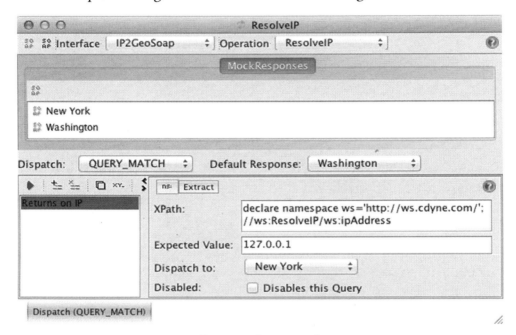

Fig. 6.14 - Query match

Script

Script dispatch is the most powerful dispatch method, but also the most complex and the less maintainable.

Scripts are written in the Groovy programming language, a dynamic language compiled to standard *bytecode* and running on the Java Virtual Machine. Such scripts can use the full range of the SoapUI API.

The following article presents a full-fledged script usage: http://www.soapui. org/Service-Mocking/creating-dynamic-mockservices.html#5-selecting-a-response-based-on-the-request.

Please refer to the SoapUI API for more capabilities.

By default, the following variables are available in the script:

- context and requestContext, both of type MockRunContext represent respectively the MockService-scoped and the MockRequest-scoped contexts
- mockRequest of type WsdlMockRequest holds a reference to the incoming request
- mockOperation of type WsdlMockOperation references the invoked operation

With these objects and SoapUI API, the previous behavior - IP 127.0.0.1 returning the "New York" response, other IPs returning the "Washington" one, can be achieved quite easily:

Code 6.10 - Groovy dispatch script sample

```
1   import com.eviware.soapui.support.GroovyUtils
2
3   def groovyUtils = new GroovyUtils(context)
4   def holder = groovyUtils.getXmlHolder(mockRequest.requestContent)
5
6   holder.declareNamespace("ws", "http://ws.cdyne.com/")
7
8   def ip = holder.getNodeValue("//ws:ResolveIP/ws:ipAddress")
9
10  mockOperation.defaultResponse = ip == "127.0.0.1" ? "New York" : "Washington"
```

 ## Keep scripting in check

As always with dynamic features, be aware of its power... and trend toward lack of maintainability. The whole response could be crafted through scripting. However, that would mean code, hence testing: testing one's testing code might be a little too much over-engineering, to says the least.

6.2.3.2 Dynamic responses

The previous section listed different dispatch methods meant to return a single response among multiple ones. However, it is also possible to return a response that is dynamic in essence.

Reasonable dynamic response use-cases include:

- A control field value in the request has to be found in the response
- A message correlation id that needs to be the same
- A message conversation index that needs to be incremented
- A search request based on a value needs that value back in the answer (*e.g.* searching for entity with id xxx needs to return an entity with this particular id and no other)

Such use-cases can be resolved through SoapUI's Property Expansion feature. Property Expansion makes it possible to insert placeholders using the ${xxx} syntax in the XML response, that can then be *expanded* at runtime by looking for similarly named attributes in the requestContext.

Using this technique, one can create a single dynamic response that will mimic the previous dispatch behavior. This requires the following XML response:

Code 6.11 - Expansion-ready XML response

```
1   <soapenv:Envelope xmlns:soapenv="http://schemas.xmlsoap.org/soap/envelope/"
2           xmlns:ws="http://ws.cdyne.com/">
3      <soapenv:Header/>
4      <soapenv:Body>
5         <ws:ResolveIPResponse>
6            <!--Optional:-->
7            <ws:ResolveIPResult>
8               <ws:City>${city}</ws:City>
9               <ws:StateProvince>${state}</ws:StateProvince>
10              <ws:Country>United States</ws:Country>
11              <ws:Organization></ws:Organization>
12              <ws:Latitude>${latitude}</ws:Latitude>
13              <ws:Longitude>${longitude}</ws:Longitude>
```

```
14                    <ws:AreaCode>0</ws:AreaCode>
15                    <ws:TimeZone />
16                    <ws:HasDaylightSavings>false</ws:HasDaylightSavings>
17                    <ws:Certainty>100</ws:Certainty>
18                    <ws:RegionName />
19                    <ws:CountryCode>US</ws:CountryCode>
20                </ws:ResolveIPResult>
21            </ws:ResolveIPResponse>
22        </soapenv:Body>
23    </soapenv:Envelope>
```

Note data common to both responses (*e.g.* Country) has not been variable-ized to be as simple as possible. At this point, the following Groovy script can be set on the response script tab (as in the Script dispatch case above):

Code 6.12 - Groovy script for Property Expansion

```
1  import com.eviware.soapui.support.GroovyUtils
2
3  def groovyUtils = new GroovyUtils(context)
4  def holder = groovyUtils.getXmlHolder(mockRequest.requestContent)
5
6  holder.declareNamespace("ws", "http://ws.cdyne.com/")
7
8  def ip = holder.getNodeValue("//ws:ResolveIP/ws:ipAddress")
9
10 if (ip == "127.0.0.1") {
11        requestContext.city = "New York"
12        requestContext.state = "NY"
13        requestContext.latitude = 40.689215
14        requestContext.longitude = -74.0445419
15
16 } else {
17        requestContext.city = "Washington"
18        requestContext.state = "CO"
19        requestContext.latitude = 38.897931
20        requestContext.longitude = -77.036527
21 }
```

This script is pretty self-explanatory: lines 1-10 are similar as those for dispatching. Only differences are requestContext.key = value statements, that let Soa)pUI set values for the different key placeholders.

6.2.4 GUI-less automated testing

In previous sections, dynamic behavior required usage of the SoapUI GUI, to create new Mock Services, Operations and Responses. However, this is not the only way to provide Mock Responses during an automated test execution. Thanks to SoapUI rich API, it is also possible to do completely without any input coming from SoapUI IDE. In this case, the WsdlProject instance is not read from the SoapUI project file but created programmatically.

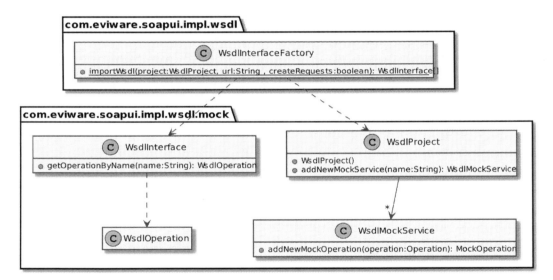

Fig. 6.15 - SoapUI GUI-less class hierarchy part 1

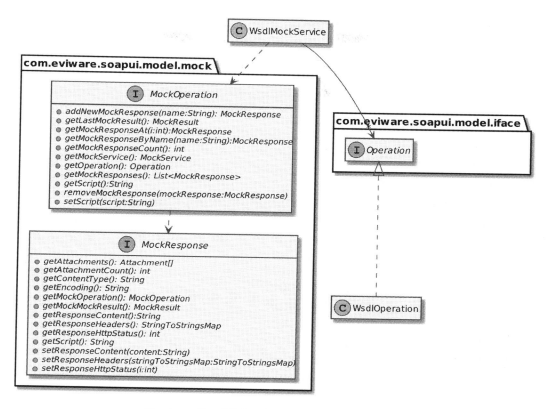

Fig. 6.16 - SoapUI GUI-less class hierarchy part 2

Some classes are already described in section Using SoapUI programmatically above, others are described next:

WsdlInterfaceFactory

WsdlInterfaceFactory implements the Factory Design Pattern to create WsdlInterface objects from a WSDL file (on disk or online) and a WsdlProject instance.

WsdlInterface

WsdlInterface represents bindings defined in the Web Service Definition (WSDL) file *e.g.* <wsdl:binding name="IP2GeoSoap" type="tns:IP2GeoSoap">

WsdlOperation

WsdlOperation represents binding operations defined in the Web Service

Definition file *e.g.* `<wsdl:operation name="ResolveIP">`

MockOperation

`WsdlOperation` wraps a `WsdlOperation` instance in the SoapUI API world. It offers access to associated `MockService` (read-only), `MockRequest` (read-only) and `MockResponse`(s) (read and write).

MockResponse

`MockResponse` represents the response returned by SoapUI. Aside from being able to evaluate the content of the associated Groovy scrpipt (if any), important methods includes accessors (all read-only, except where noted):

- the content, as used in the above example (read and write)
- encoding
- content type
- the HTTP status (read and write)
- response headers (read and write)
- the script (read and write)
- attachments array and as an helper, attachement count

As an illustration, here is the setup code that creates a static response whatever the request, for the IP2Geo SOAP web service:

Code 6.13 - Static method return Fake Service sample

```
1   @BeforeClass
2   protected void setUpBeforeClass() throws Exception {
3       WsdlProject project = new WsdlProject();
4       String wsdlFile = "file:src/test/resources/chapter6/ip2geo.wsdl";
5       WsdlInterface wsdlInterface = importWsdl(project, wsdlFile, true)[0];
6       WsdlMockService fakeService = project.addNewMockService("fakeService");
7       WsdlOperation wsdlOp = wsdlInterface.getOperationByName("ResolveIP");
8       MockOperation fakeOp = fakeService.addNewMockOperation(wsdlOp);
9       MockResponse fakeResp = fakeOp.addNewMockResponse("fakeResponse");
10      fakeResp.setResponseContent("<soapenv:Envelope>...</soapenv:Envelope>");
11      runner = fakeService.start();
12  }
13
```

```
14   @Test
15   public void should_always_return_new_york() throws Exception {
16       URL url = new URL("http://localhost:8080/ip2geo/ip2geo.asmx?wsdl");
17       QName qName = new QName("http://ws.cdyne.com/", "IP2Geo");
18       Service service = Service.create(url, qName);
19       IP2GeoSoap port = service.getPort(IP2GeoSoap.class);
20       IPInformation result = port.resolveIP("127.0.0.1", "dummyKey");
21       assertEquals(result.city, "New York");
22       assertEquals(result.stateProvince, "NY");
23       assertEquals(result.country, "United States");
24       assertEquals(result.latitude, 40.689215);
25       assertEquals(result.longitude, -74.0445419);
26   }
27
28   @AfterClass
29   protected void tearDownAfterClass() {
30       if (runner != null & runner.isRunning()) {
31           runner.stop();
32       }
33   }
34   }
```

Line 5

The WsdlInterfaceFactory.importWsdl() method creates a WsdlInterface instance, using information read from the WSDL file and binding it to the WsdlProject instantiated at line 4.

Line 6

A new MockService is added on the WsdlProject. The only required parameter is its name.

Line 7

A WsdlOperation is read by its name from the WsdlInterface object, as the latter has been injected with all WSDL data in line 8.

Line 8

A new MockOperation is added on the WsdlProject from an existing WSDL operation.

Line 9

As for `MockService` on the `WsdlProject`, a new `MockResponse`is added on the `MockOperation`.

Line 10

`MockResponse` content is set. Once the server is started (on line 20), this set content will be returned each time the SOAP operation is called.

 GUI-less testing can be used for Property Expansion as well as for Dynamic Dispatch

6.3 Summary

This chapter has been entirely dedicated to Faking web service resources.

The first part revolved around REST architecture web services. REST resources can easily be faked using the Spark web framework. Spark offers a very simple API to serve resources when requested with a specific path. It is easy as pie to create a route to serve a resource.

The second part covered SOAP web services. As opposed to REST, SOAP is much more strict and standardized: in order to fake SOAP resources, a dedicated tool was required - SoapUI. SoapUI is more complex to setup but offers many features such as dynamic responses and dispatch.

The next chapter will describe the next level of integration testing, in-container testing.

7. Spring in-container testing

One aspect of Spring Test has already been mentioned in *Chapter 3 - Test-Friendly Design* as a way to help in Integration Testing by providing ready- to-use Fakes. However, Spring framework's main usage is geared towards dependency injection.

Up to now, Integration Testing has been about testing collaboration of classes, regardless of how they are assembled in the running system. This approach has its limits, as the way of assembling classes might be different across tests and the running system. However, most current applications need to be run inside a container. This container provides services so that applications only have to call them, instead of redeveloping them from scratch for every new application. Spring is such a container, along with the Java EE platform. In order to improve confidence in integration tests, using the "real" container (the one used in production) as a testing platform is required.

This chapter tries to detail techniques and tools that help to bridge this gap::

- First, how to easily manage Spring dependencies with the Maven build system will be described.
- Then, the three different Spring styles of configuration - XML, Autowiring and JavaConfig - are going to be detailed
- We will have a look at tools aimed at making Integration Testing Spring and Spring web applications based on Spring MVC a breeze.

To complete the chapter, a section will be dedicated to a case study on how to do Integration Testing on the famed and classic Spring Pet Clinic application.

7.1 Spring dependencies management

From its inception, the Spring framework has been broken down into different modules including Spring Test, Spring MVC and others, so that developers can use only the modules necessary for their application.

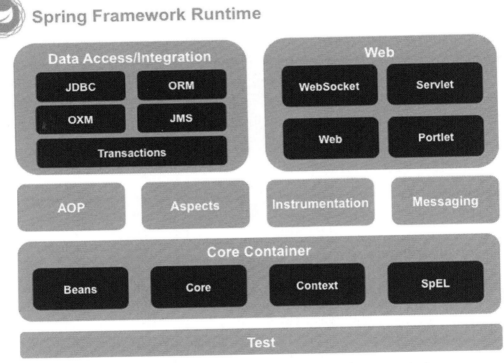

Fig. 7.1 - Spring modules overview (taken from Spring documentation)

While not specific to Integration Testing, this section covers ways to manage Spring dependencies more easily.

7.1.1 Using Spring and Spring Platform BOMs

Modularization is good, but it is of utmost importance that in the context of a single application, all dependent Spring modules depicted above have the exact same version to ensure compatibility. As seen in *Chapter 4 - Automated testing*, the Spring framework provides a Bill of Material POM to easily achieve this.

 Astute readers may think Maven's transitive dependencies management (http://maven.apache.org/guides/introduction/introduction-to-dependency-mechanism.html#Transitive_Dependencies) is enough. However, transitivity is only applied to modules that are not dependencies (*e.g.* Spring Test and Spring JDBC).

To use this BOM, just use the following snippet:

Code 7.1 - Example Spring POM file using Spring's BOM

```
1   <?xml version="1.0" encoding="UTF-8"?>
2   <project ...>
3       <modelVersion>4.0.0</modelVersion>
4       <groupId>org.integrationtest</groupId>
5       <artifactId>spring-sample</artifactId>
6       <version>1.0</version>
7       <dependencyManagement>
8           <dependencies>
9               <dependency>
10                  <groupId>org.springframework</groupId>
11                  <artifactId>spring-framework-bom</artifactId>
12                  <type>pom</type>
13                  <version>4.0.5.RELEASE</version>
14                  <scope>import</scope>
15              </dependency>
16          </dependencies>
17      </dependencyManagement>
18      <dependencies>
19          <dependency>
20              <groupId>org.springframework</groupId>
```

```
21            <artifactId>spring-test</artifactId>
22          </dependency>
23          <dependency>
24              <groupId>org.springframework</groupId>
25              <artifactId>spring-webmvc</artifactId>
26          </dependency>
27            . . .
28        </dependencies>
29   </project>
```

During the writing of this book, Spring released the Spring IO platform, which includes a BOM (https://github.com/spring-io/platform/blob/master/platform-bom/pom.xml). The POM's hierarchy looks like the following:

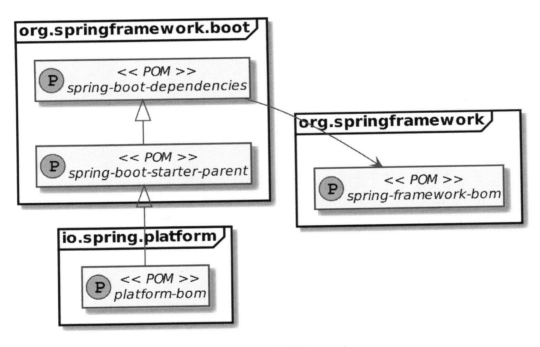

Fig. 7.2 - Spring BOM hierarchy

This BOM references not only Spring modules, but also a bunch of common third-party libraries (including libraries seen previously such as TestNG, Mockito and h2). It ensures all referenced libraries have versions compatible with one another, a common challenge in any real-world application. The following POM is an example of how Spring IO platform can be leveraged to guarantee version compatibilities across libraries:

Code 7.2 - Example Spring POM file using Spring IO platform's BOM

```
1   <?xml version="1.0" encoding="UTF-8"?>
2   <project ...>
3       <modelVersion>4.0.0</modelVersion>
4       <groupId>org.integrationtest</groupId>
5       <artifactId>spring-sample</artifactId>
6       <version>1.0</version>
7       <dependencyManagement>
8           <dependencies>
9               <dependency>
10                  <groupId>io.spring.platform</groupId>
11                  <artifactId>platform-bom</artifactId>
12                  <type>pom</type>
13                  <version>1.0.0.RELEASE</version>
14                  <scope>import</scope>
15              </dependency>
16          </dependencies>
17      </dependencyManagement>
18      <dependencies>
19          <dependency>
20              <groupId>org.springframework</groupId>
21              <artifactId>spring-webmvc</artifactId>
22          </dependency>
23          <dependency>
24              <groupId>org.testng</groupId>
25              <artifactId>testng</artifactId>
26              <scope>test</scope>
27          </dependency>
28      </dependencies>
29  </project>
```

The above POM imports Spring IO platform BOM and declares dependencies on

Spring MVC and TestNG; as the BOM has been imported, setting versions on depen-dencies is not mandatory (and since versions are guaranteed to be compatible, also not recommended). In this particular case, note that BOM version 1.0.0.RELEASE defines versions 4.0.5.RELEASE and 6.8.8 of Spring MVC and TestNG respectively. However, there is no simple rule to determine one from the other, the only option is to look into a particular BOM version and its hierarchy.

Note the Spring BOM only defines versions, not scope: it is up to the user to configure the scope, when needed (as shown above).

And Gradle?

Gradle users should check the documentation (https://github.com/spring-gradle-plugins/dependency-management-plugin#importing-a-maven-bom) of Spring's dependency management plugin for Gradle .

7.2 Spring configuration modularization

The basics of Integration Testing requires defining the System Under Test (SUT) and its dependencies, which need to be either mocked or faked as seen in previous chapters. The Spring framework is based on the notion of contexts which hold bean definitions. Those beans represent instances of classes used by the application: web controllers, services, data sources and so on.

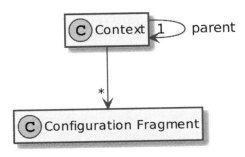

Fig. 7.3 - Spring contexts and configuration fragments

Enabling Integration Testing requires segregating beans that are part of the SUT and beans that are not into different configuration fragments, so the latter can be switched depending on the environment.

Managing configuration fragments depends on how the Spring application is configured. Configuration comes in three different flavors:

1. XML-based configuration
2. JavaConfig
3. Autowiring configuration

 The configuration style can be mixed and matched, though it is far from recommended. Enabling Integration Testing will be described only for "pure" configuration style.

7.2.1 XML configuration fragments

Originally, XML configuration was the only way to configure Spring applications. Here is an example of such a configuration file:

Code 7.3 - Example Spring XML configuration file

```
1  <?xml version="1.0" encoding="UTF-8"?>
2  <beans xmlns="http://www.springframework.org/schema/beans"
3         xmlns:jee="http://www.springframework.org/schema/jee"
4         xmlns:xsi="http://www.w3.org/2001/XMLSchema-instance"
5         xsi:schemaLocation="http://www.springframework.org/schema/beans
6             http://www.springframework.org/schema/beans/spring-beans.xsd
7             http://www.springframework.org/schema/jee
8             http://www.springframework.org/schema/jee/spring-jee.xsd">
9      <jee:jndi-lookup id="dataSource" jndi-name="jdbc/MyDataSource" />
10     <bean id="productRepository" class="chapter7.ProductRepository">
11         <constructor-arg ref="dataSource" />
12     </bean>
13     <bean id="customerRepository" class="chapter7.CustomerRepository">
```

```
14            <constructor-arg ref="dataSource" />
15        </bean>
16    </beans>
```

This configuration is simple but requires a JNDI datasource, a common occurence in enterprises. It is meant to run inside an application server with JNDI capabilities. Although this is possible (as will be seen in the *Chapter 9 - Java EE Testing*), it would require much effort in downloading and setting up a Java EE container for just Integration Testing. A JNDI datasource is an infrastructure resource, and as seen in *Chapter 5 - Infrastructure Resources Integration*, there are ways to fake such resources. With Spring, this only requires breaking down the XML configuration file into two different fragments, one dedicated to the datasource and taking advantage of Maven class path management, as test resources (target/test-classes) are set *earlier* on the classpath than main's (target/classes).

In order to do this, the required steps are as follows:

- Move the dataSource bean into a different file
- Duplicate the file, and put one into src/main/resoures and the other into src/test/resources
- In the second file, change the dataSource bean type
- Finally, import the data source config file from the main config file

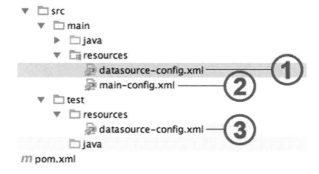

Fig. 7.4 - Modular Spring configuration XML files layout

1. This is just the data source bean, put into its own configuration file.

Code 7.4 - src/main/resources/datasource-config.xml

```
1   <?xml version="1.0" encoding="UTF-8"?>
2   <beans ...>
3       <jee:jndi-lookup id="dataSource" jndi-name="jdbc/MyDataSource" />
4   </beans>
```

2. Likewise, these are repository beans put into their dedicated configuration file.

Code 7.5 - main-config.xml

```
1    <?xml version="1.0" encoding="UTF-8"?>
2    <beans ...>
3        <import resource="classpath:datasource-config.xml" />
4        <bean id="productRepository" class="chapter7.ProductRepository">
5            <constructor-arg ref="dataSource" />
6        </bean>
7        <bean id="customerRepository" class="chapter7.CustomerRepository">
8            <constructor-arg ref="dataSource" />
9        </bean>
10   </beans>
```

3. A configuration file for the testing data source only. In a local environment, a standard direct connection to the database can be used, it just has to be wrapped inside a DataSource adapter. An adequate adapter is Tomcat DBCP's org.apache.tomcat.jdbc.pool.DataSource. For an alternative, check C3P0 (http://www.mchange.com/projects/c3p0/), a mature connection pooling library.

Code 7.6 - src/test/resources/datasource-config.xml

```xml
1   <?xml version="1.0" encoding="UTF-8"?>
2   <beans ...>
3       <bean id="dataSource" class="org.apache.tomcat.jdbc.pool.DataSource">
4           <property name="driverClassName" value="org.h2.Driver" />
5           <property name="url"            value="jdbc:h2:~/test" />
6           <property name="username"       value="sa" />
7           <property name="maxActive"      value="1" />
8       </bean>
9   </beans>
```

 # Pool starvation testing

Web application generally use connection pools: application servers are configured to request a set of them at startup time. This prevents requesting an SQL database connection each time one is required, which causes performance bottlenecks. At runtime, data access code gets one from the pool, uses it and releases it immediately afterwards.

A common mistake when using connection pools is for code to "forget" to release. At some point, the pool is exhausted and no new connections can be retrieved from the pool. This widespread phenomenon is commonly known as *connection pool starvation* or *connection pool exhaustion*.

In order to detect this problem before the production environment and ensure a robust coding practice, the test data source **must** be configured with only a single active connection (hence the `maxActive` set to 1 in the previous snippet) so that the pool gets exhausted just afer the faulty code. Note that `org.springframework.jdbc.datasource.AbstractDriverBasedDataSource` and its subclasses cannot help testing pool exhaustion.

As both data source config files have the same name, the file in `src/test/resources` will be taken in priority over the one in `src/main/resources`, as the former is set *earlier* on the classpath.

Though effective, the previous solution has several downsides:

- It relies on Maven's classpath management
- It relies on files having exactly the same path and name
- It strongly couples the relationship between XML fragments as they are referenced in the `<import>` tag

A better alternative moves the responsiblity of aggregating the different configuration fragment files from the main configuration file to the code itself. This is done differently depending on the exact situation. Here is a summary of the different possible situations:

Standalone

This situation happens when one creates the container programmatically. This is rare as most use-cases nowadays involve a web application, but it deserves a mention nonetheless. Using multiple configuration fragments is achieved with the following snippet:

```
ApplicationContext ctx = new FileSystemXmlApplicationContext(
        "classpath:main-config.xml", "classpath:datasource-config.xml");
```

Web application

Spring Web applications are very widespread and represent the most common use-cases. In this situation, the Spring framework create one "main" context, and one web context for each Dispatcher servlet, dedicated to servlet configuration and controllers. Using multiple configuration fragments is achieved through web deployment descriptor configuration.

Code 7.7 - Sample web deployment descriptor configured for multiple configuration fragments

```
1  <web-app xmlns="http://java.sun.com/xml/ns/javaee"
2           xmlns:xsi="http://www.w3.org/2001/XMLSchema-instance"
3           xsi:schemaLocation="http://java.sun.com/xml/ns/javaee
4           http://java.sun.com/xml/ns/javaee/web-app_3_0.xsd" version="3.0">
5      <servlet>
6          <servlet-name>dispatcher</servlet-name>
7          <servlet-class>
8              org.springframework.web.servlet.DispatcherServlet
9          </servlet-class>
```

```
10        <init-param>
11            <param-name>contextConfigLocation</param-name>
12            <param-value>
13                /WEB-INF/dispatcher-servlet.xml
14                /WEB-INF/another-config.xml
15            </param-value>
16        </init-param>
17    </servlet>
18    <servlet-mapping>
19        <servlet-name>dispatcher</servlet-name>
20        <url-pattern>/*</url-pattern>
21    </servlet-mapping>
22    <context-param>
23        <param-name>contextConfigLocation</param-name>
24        <param-value>
25            classpath:config/applicationContext.xml
26            classpath:config/anotherConfig.xml
27        </param-value>
28    </context-param>
29    <listener>
30        <listener-class>
31            org.springframework.web.context.ContextLoaderListener
32        </listener-class>
33    </listener>
34 </web-app>
```

This snippet describes the following structure:

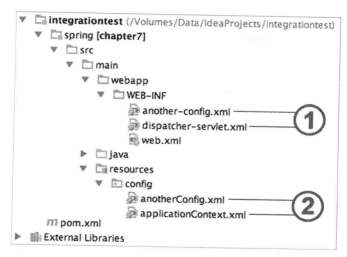

Fig. 7.5 - Spring web project configuration XML files layout

1. Spring web context XML configuration fragments
2. Spring main context XML configuration fragments

Tests

Last but not least, tests (whether unit or integration) are the last place where configuration fragments can be assembled. This will be described in the section Spring Test below.

7.2.2 JavaConfig fragments

In recent years, JavaConfig has been provided as an alternative to XML and autowiring, getting the best of both worlds - compile-time safety as well as bean/class decoupling. In short, instead of an XML file, there is a corresponding Java class annotated with @Configuration and for each <bean> tag, there is a corresponding method annotated with @Bean. The following class is equivalent to code 7.1 above.

Code 7.8 - Sample Spring JavaConfig configuration

```
1    import org.springframework.context.annotation.*;
2
3    import javax.naming.*;
4    import javax.sql.DataSource;
5
6    @Configuration
7    public class MonolithicJavaConfig {
8
9        @Bean
10       public DataSource dataSource() throws Exception {
11           Context ctx = new InitialContext();
12           return (DataSource) ctx.lookup("jdbc/MyDataSource");
13       }
14
15       @Bean
16       public ProductRepository productRepository() throws Exception {
17           return new ProductRepository(dataSource());
18       }
19
20       @Bean
21       public CustomerRepository customerRepository() throws Exception {
22           return new CustomerRepository(dataSource());
23       }
24   }
```

As with XML, this sample is a monolithic JavaConfig class, not adapted to Integration Testing purposes. Likewise, the dataSource() bean needs to be put into its own configuration class and the two configuration fragments have to be assembled. Here is the code for the Fake data source, equivalent to its XML counterpart seen above in code 7.7:

Code 7.9 - Fake data source JavaConfig fragment

```
1   import javax.sql.DataSource;
2
3   public class FakeDataSourceConfig {
4
5       public DataSource dataSource() {
6           org.apache.tomcat.jdbc.pool.DataSource dataSource =
7               new org.apache.tomcat.jdbc.pool.DataSource();
8           dataSource.setDriverClassName("org.h2.Driver");
9           dataSource.setUrl("jdbc:h2:~/test");
10          dataSource.setUsername("sa");
11          dataSource.setMaxActive(1);
12          return dataSource;
13      }
14  }
```

The JavaConfig class still needs to compile and therefore a reference to the data source bean is required so it can be injected in the repository beans. In order for beans in one configuration fragment class to be referenced in another configuration fragment class, they need to be autowired in the latter class with the help of the @Autowired annotation.

Code 7.10 - Modular Spring JavaConfig configuration

```
1   import org.springframework.beans.factory.annotation.Autowired;
2   import org.springframework.context.annotation.*;
3
4   import javax.sql.DataSource;
5
6   @Configuration
7   public class MainConfig {
8
9       @Autowired
10      private DataSource dataSource;
11
12      @Bean
```

```
13      public ProductRepository productRepository() throws Exception {
14          return new ProductRepository(dataSource);
15      }
16
17      @Bean
18      public CustomerRepository customerRepository() throws Exception {
19          return new CustomerRepository(dataSource);
20      }
21  }
```

As with XML fragments, it is the caller's responsibility - whether application or test - to assemble the different configuration fragments.

```
ApplicationContext ctx = new AnnotationConfigApplicationContext(
    MainConfig.class, DataSourceConfig.class);
```

7.2.2.1 No web deployment descriptor

Since Servlet 3.0, a web deployment descriptor is not mandatory . At context startup, the Spring container scans for all classes implementing WebApplicationInitializer. Spring provides such an implementation with the AbstractAnnotationConfigDispatcherServletInitializer. Mandatory methods to implement are:

- getRootConfigClasses() to specify all configuration fragment classes for the main context
- getServletConfigClasses() to return all configuration fragment classes for the web context
- getServletMappings() to configure all servlet mappings

The equivalent class to the above web.xml is the following:

Code 7.11 - Sample web initializer configured for multiple configuration fragment classes

```
1   import o.s.w.s.support.AbstractAnnotationConfigDispatcherServletInitializer;
2
3   public class DispatcherServletInitializer
4       extends AbstractAnnotationConfigDispatcherServletInitializer {
5
6       @Override
7       protected Class<?>[] getRootConfigClasses() {
8           return new Class<?>[]
9               { ApplicationContextConfig.class, AnotherConfig.class };
10      }
11
12      @Override
13      protected Class<?>[] getServletConfigClasses() {
14          return new Class<?>[]
15              { DispatcherServletConfig.class, AnotherWebConfig.class };
16      }
17
18      @Override
19      protected String[] getServletMappings() {
20          return new String[] { "/*" };
21      }
22  }
```

7.2.2.2 Profiles

As an improvement to configuration modularization, Spring also provides the proprietary @Profile annotation.

 Profiles are also available in XML, but as JavaConfig is the preferred way of configuring Spring applications, interested readers are encouraged to read the online documentation: https://spring.io/blog/2011/02/11/spring-framework-3-1-m1-released/.

In the previous section, assembler code needs to know which fragments are required for the test. Profiles make it possible to assemble all fragments indiscriminately, but in a way that each individual bean might be activated (or not) by a dedicated profile. Basically, a profile is just a label set on a bean **and/or** a configuration class, after which activating the profile will add the bean to the context, and not activating it will not. Annotating a configuration class with @Profile will bind all beans of that configuration class to the said profile, while annotating a specific bean-returning method will expectedly bind that bean to the profile. **Annotating both class and method will require both profiles to be activated** for the bean to be made available.

Code 7.12 - Bean profile binding

```
1    import org.springframework.context.annotation.*;
2
3    @Configuration
4    @Profile("development")
5    public class ProfileConfig {
6
7        @Bean
8        public Object bean1() { ... }
9
10       @Bean
11       @Profile("anotherProfile")
12       public Object bean2() { ... }
13
14       @Bean
15       @Profile("thirdProfile")
16       public Object bean3() { ... }
17   }
```

Creating more robust profiles

The previous way of binding a bean to a profile is somewhat fragile as it relies on a string. A much more robust and type-safe way of achieving the same result is to create a dedicated annotation for this.

Code 7.13 - Robust bean profile binding

```
1   import org.springframework.context.annotation.Profile;
2
3   import java.lang.annotation.*;
4
5   import static java.lang.annotation.ElementType.TYPE;
6   import static java.lang.annotation.RetentionPolicy.RUNTIME;
7
8   @Profile("development")
9   @Retention(RUNTIME)
10  @Target(TYPE)
11  public @interface DevelopmentProfile { }
```

At this point, line 4 of snippet 7.12 above can be replaced as shown here:

```
3   @Configuration
4   @DevelopmentProfile
5   public class ProfileConfig { ... }
```

Here is the result of activating a profile on bean availability in the context:

Table 7.1 - Profile/bean activation matrix

Profile	bean1	bean2	bean3
None			
development	X		
anotherProfile			
development && anotherProfile	X	X	
development && thirdProfile	X		X

7.2.2.3 Profile activation

There are multiple ways of activating profiles:

Through a system property

Mostly used for standalone Spring applications, profiles can be activated through the `spring.profiles.active` system property on the command-line.

```
java -Dspring.profiles.active="development,anotherProfile" \
                                            MySpringApplication
```

 Using a system property for web applications will activate the same profile(s) for **all** web applications on the same application server for they share the same JVM. Therefore, one must take care before choosing this option. Most of the time, it will be wiser to choose one of the other options.

Programmatically

The programmatic way is the most straightforward for activating profiles. At runtime, profiles are stored in a Spring abstraction called an *environment*. Here is a class diagram summarizing all collaborating classes.

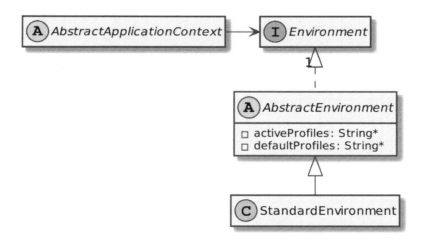

Fig. 7.6 - Environment class diagram

Activating profiles programmatically is as easy as the following lines:

```
ApplicationContext ctx = new AnnotationConfigApplicationContext(...)
ctx.getEnvironment().setActiveProfiles("development", "anotherProfile");
```

🔑 Activating profiles with code in a web application

In the above snippet, the returned environment is of type `ConfigurableEnvironment` which supports the `setActiveProfiles()` method. However, the `WebApplicationContext` interface returns a simple `Environment` abstraction which does not support it. This requires casting the environment reference to a `ConfigurableEnvironment` first.

```
WebApplicationContext ctx =
 WebApplicationContextUtils.getRequiredWebApplicationContext(servletContext);
ConfigurableEnvironment env = (ConfigurableEnvironment) ctx.getEnvironment();
env.setActiveProfiles("development", "anotherProfile");
```

Web Applications

As seen in the web application initializer above (see code 7.8), web applications have multiple contexts, one main context and one web application context per Dispatcher servlet.

- The main context can be configured through the development of a custom `ApplicationContextInitializer` implementation. The single `initialize(String...)` method offers a reference to the `ConfigurableApplicationContext` instance. The latter provides a `getEnvironment()` method from where active profiles can be set.

Code 7.14 - Setting profiles on the main context

```
1   import org.springframework.context.*;
2
3   public class MainContextInitializer
4     implements ApplicationContextInitializer<ConfigurableApplicationContext> {
5
6       @Override
7       public void initialize(ConfigurableApplicationContext context) {
8           context.getEnvironment().setActiveProfiles(
9               "development", "anotherProfile");
10      }
11  }
```

- Web contexts are bound to a servlet. Activating profiles for such a web
  context is achieved by overriding the customizeRegistration() method
  on the AbstractAnnotationConfigDispatcherServletInitializer and
  calling the setInitParameter() method on the provided
  ServletRegistration.Dynamic parameter:

Code 7.15 - Setting profiles on a web context

```
1   import o.s.w.s.s.AbstractAnnotationConfigDispatcherServletInitializer;
2
3   import static javax.servlet.ServletRegistration.Dynamic;
4
5   public class DispatcherServletInitializer
6       extends AbstractAnnotationConfigDispatcherServletInitializer {
7
8       @Override
9       protected void customizeRegistration(Dynamic registration) {
10          registration.setInitParameter("spring.profiles.active",
11                                        "development");
12      }
13      ...
14  }
```

In a test

Profiles can be activated on a per-test class basis through the @ActiveProfiles annotation. It will be described in more detail in the section Spring Test below.

7.2.2.4 Default profiles

Default profiles are profiles that are active when no other profile is activated. They can be set in the same way as active profiles but replacing spring.profiles.active by spring.profiles.default. The usual use-case is to have two data source beans bound to a profile: a production one and a development one. The former profile is set as default so that it will be active in the final product, the latter is activated on a case-by-case basis when required, during tests or development.

Here's an illustration:

```
public class MainContextInitializer
    implements ApplicationContextInitializer<ConfigurableApplicationContext> {

    @Override
    public void initialize(ConfigurableApplicationContext context) {
        context.getEnvironment().setDefaultProfiles("production");
    }
}

@ContextConfiguration(classes = ...)
@ActiveProfiles("development")
public class ProfileTest extends AbstractTestNGSpringContextTests {
    ...
}
```

The MainContextInitializer class sets a default profile which will be used in all executions where no profiles have been set. However, in the ProfileTest test class just above, the development profile is set so that beans associated to the development profile will be created and beans associated to the production will not.

Alternative web.xml configuration

Instead of Java code, it is also possible to activate profiles within the web.xml deployment descriptor. As above, there are two different ways depending on the type of the context (main or web).

- The main context is configured through the `<context-param>` tag. Activating a profile for the main context requires such a tag with a `<param-name>` value of `spring.profiles.active`

```xml
<context-param>
    <param-name>spring.profiles.active</param-name>
    <param-value>development</param-value>
</context-param>
```

- Web contexts are bound to a servlet. Activating a profile for such a web context basis is achieved through a `spring.profiles.active` `<init-param>` tag on the servlet.

```xml
<servlet>
    <servlet-name>dispatcher</servlet-name>
    <servlet-class>
        org.springframework.web.servlet.DispatcherServlet
    </servlet-class>
    <init-param>
        <param-name>spring.profiles.active</param-name>
        <param-value>development</param-value>
    </init-param>
</servlet>
```

7.2.3 Autowiring and modularization

When it was introduced, autowiring was designed as an improvement over XML configuration. However, autowiring requires dependency injection not to be explicit, but instead relies on the Spring container to find **one bean and only one** to match the dependency requirement. This is the reason why it is sometimes said that autowiring fills dependencies *auto-magically*.

Autowiring's single bean rule can be summarized as the Highlander (http://en.wikipedia.org/wiki/Highlander)'s rule since *there can be only one!*

When using autowiring, one must avoid attribute autowiring in favour of constructor autowiring in order to be able to painlessly inject mocks in unit tests.

```java
// This prevents easy injection during tests
public class InjectedBean {

    @Autowired
    private MyType myObject;
    ...
}

// This allows injection during tests
public class InjectedBean {

    private MyType myObject;

    @Autowired
    public InjectedBean(MyType myObject) {
        this.myObject = myObject;
    }
    ...
}

public class InjectedBeanTest {

    private InjectedBean beanUnderTest;

    @BeforeMethod
    protected void setUp() {
        MyType myObject = new MyType();
        beanUnderTest = new InjectedBean(myObject);
    }
    ...
}
```

Integration Testing and autowiring

Integration Testing an autowired-configured piece of code is several levels of magnitude harder to achieve than with XML or JavaConfig. As seen above, XML/JavaConfig configuration can be broken down into different fragments so they can be assembled for Integration Testing. On the other hand, autowiring relies on component scanning. To do the same with autowiring, one has to choose which classes must be scanned, and by keeping the same configuration, this is only possible when one chooses classes that are deployed.

While this can be leveraged by using Shrinkwrap to package those classes in conjunction with Arquillian to deploy it to an application server (both of them will be seen in *Chapter 9 - Java EE testing*), it is advised to migrate to either XML or JavaConfig configuration type.

7.2.4 Configuration parameterization

Many applications require different configuration for each environment:

- local
- local test
- deployed in integration
- deployed in production
- etc.

Also, some specific designs also require *per-developer* configuration. One classic example is the usage of a remote oracle schema for each developer on the team, as described previously in *Chapter 5 - Infrastructure Resources Integration*.

In both cases, this requires the configuration(s) to be parameterizable. The first use-case - configuration per environment - has already been resolved by modularizing configuration into configuration fragments. The second use-case might be resolved the same way: each developer creates a dedicated Spring configuration file that won't be committed into the SCM (Source Control Management) tool. However, this approache has at least two disadvantages:

1. As the fragment(s) are not under SCM, each developer has to either create the fragment from scratch, or get a copy from a colleague and change it for his own use.
2. More importantly, if JavaConfig is used, that means that code will **not** compile until the fragment has been developed.

7.2.4.1 Properties

A much better alternative is to have a single fragment structure - XML or JavaConfig, and version it in the SCM, while putting values in an external properties file that can be kept locally. For this, Spring provides the `@PropertySource` annotation that takes the path to the properties file as its value. It has to be set on the configuration class:

```
@PropertySource("classpath:parameters.properties")
@Configuration
public class PropertyConfig {

    ...

}
```

Note the `classpath:` prefix - since the value is a string, and basically the file can be anywhere, Spring has conventions for acceptable locations:

- The `classpath:` prefix defines a specific location on the class path However, this syntax will only reference the first matching resource. In order to reference all resources present as-is on the classpath and in available JARs, use the `classpath*:` prefix (notes the *).
- The `file:` prefix references an absolute path on the file system:

      file:/var/apps/myapp/config/parameters.properties
      file:D:/config/parameters.properties

- Finally, no prefix hints at a relative location:

      /WEB-INF/config/parameters.properties

Note that all paths accept Ant-style patterns, such as `classpath:*-beans.xml`. However, remember that searching for properties this way may have unintended side-effects during the life of the application (and especially after some years have passed when all original developers have left).

Property values can be used - either in standard application code or in testing code - via the @Value annotation on attributes. It takes the property key surrounded by ${ and } as its value, and Spring will set the attribute value to the value of the property in the properties file. As an example, take the following parameters.properties file in the src/test/resources folder:

Code 7.16 - Simple Oracle remote database connection parameters

```
1   dataSource.driverClassName=oracle.jdbc.OracleDriver
2   dataSource.url=jdbc:oracle:thin:@127.0.0.1:1521
3   dataSource.schema=mysid
4   dataSource.username=sa
5   dataSource.password=password
```

A typical Java configuration class using this properties file would look like this:

Code 7.17 - Java configuration class using properties

```
1   import org.springframework.beans.factory.annotation.Value;
2   import org.springframework.context.annotation.*;
3   import o.s.context.support.PropertySourcesPlaceholderConfigurer;
4
5   import org.apache.tomcat.jdbc.pool.DataSource;
6
7   @Configuration
8   @PropertySource("classpath:parameters.properties")
9   public class PropertyConfig {
10
11      @Value("${dataSource.driverClassName}")
12      private String driverClassName;
13
```

```
14      @Value("${dataSource.url}")
15      private String url;
16
17      @Value("${dataSource.schema}")
18      private String schema;
19
20      @Value("${dataSource.username}")
21      private String username;
22
23      @Value("${dataSource.password}")
24      private String password;
25
26      @Bean
27      public javax.sql.DataSource dataSource() {
28          DataSource dataSource = new DataSource();
29          dataSource.setDriverClassName(driverClassName);
30          dataSource.setUrl(url + ":" + schema);
31          dataSource.setUsername(username);
32          dataSource.setPassword(password);
33          return dataSource;
34      }
35
36      @Bean
37      public static PropertySourcesPlaceholderConfigurer placeholdConfig() {
38          return new PropertySourcesPlaceholderConfigurer();
39      }
40  }
```

 # PropertySourcesPlaceholderConfigurer

Annotating the configuration class with @PropertySource is not enough to get values injected. The Spring framework requires a bean of type PropertySourcesPlaceholderConfigurer to be registered in the context. Moreover, the method registering the bean **must** be static in order not to interfere with other annotation processors. This is the reason for lines 36-39 above.

Dependency injection is a good way to increase unit testability by providing an adequate design. In the above code, though, it adds nothing but verbosity. However, there is an alternative advocated by Spring since version 3.1. This version adds the notion of environment (as seen above) and the PropertySourcesPlaceholderConfigurer binds associated properties to the current Environment. Thus, the previous snippet can be replaced with the following:

Code 7.18 - Alternative Java configuration class for properties

```
7   @Configuration
8   @PropertySource("classpath:parameters.properties")
9   public class AlternativePropertyConfig {
10
11  @Autowired
12  private Environment env;
13
14  @Bean
15  public javax.sql.DataSource dataSource() {
16          DataSource dataSource = new DataSource();
17          dataSource.setDriverClassName(
18              env.getProperty("dataSource.driverClassName"));
19          dataSource.setUrl(env.getProperty("dataSource.url")
20                  + ":" + env.getProperty("dataSource.schema"));
21          dataSource.setUsername(env.getProperty("dataSource.username"));
22          dataSource.setPassword(env.getProperty("dataSource.password"));
23          return dataSource;
24  }
```

Finally, note that in the above configuration, some values will be the same regardless of the developer (driver and datasource) while some will be different from developer to developer (schema, user and password). Managing all of these as properties might be overkill. Spring offers an overloaded getProperty() method to have default values so that property files can only have the required properties but still be overridden if necessary:

```
env.getProperty("dataSource.driverClassName", "oracle.jdbc.OracleDriver");
```

7.3 Spring Test

Spring Test is a module that is part of the Spring framework. It is available at http://
docs.spring.io/spring/docs/current/spring-framework-reference/html/testing.html. It
provides the following features:

- Fake classes covering most of the Java EE API. These were already described
  in detail in *Chapter 3 - Test-Friendly Design.*
- Support for testing Spring MVC controllers at the URL mappings level, which
  is covered in *Chapter 8 - Spring Web MVC testing*
- Integration support with the JUnit and TestNG testing frameworks. These
  frameworks have already been detailed, please refer to *Chapter 2 - Developer
  testing tools* for a refresher if needed.
- Support for injecting context beans on test classes.

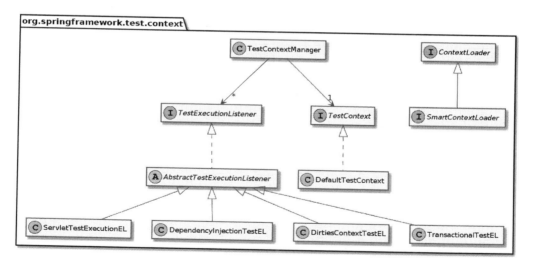

Fig. 7.7 - Spring Test class diagram

Note: for readability purposes, the above class names have been abridged from
`<Xxx>ExecutionListener` *to* `<Xxx>EL`.

TestContext

Abstraction over the text context, regardless of the actual testing framework used. It contains the actual Spring context hierarchy, the test class, the test method and the thrown exception (if any).

TestContextManager

Entry-point into the Spring Test framework. It sends messages events to its list of `TestExecutionListener` instances during the test execution lifecycle.

TestExecutionListener

`TestExecutionListener` are observers of the text execution lifecycle. They are sent messages at key phases of the test execution. The following listeners are registered by default:

- `DependencyInjectionTestExecutionListener` is responsible for injecting dependencies into the test class
- `DirtiesContextTestExecutionListener` manages tests (either methods or classes) annotated with `@DirtiesContext`

     A test annotated with `@DirtiesContext` tells the Spring framework the the execution of the test has somehow modified (*i.e.* dirtied) the Spring context, and that it needs to recreate it from scratch for the next test execution. While recreating the context if it has been dirtied is a good thing, dirtying it in the first place is bad. Beware that dirtying the context should not happen under normal circumstances: one should first question this behavior before using this feature.

- `ServletTestExecutionListener` adds Web support if the configured context if of type Web

SmartContextLoader

The `SmartContextLoader` class is responsible for loading all configured configuration fragments, whatever their nature (XML or JavaConfig). It is also in charge of activating profiles.

7.3.1 Basics

Using Spring Test is easy but depends on the underlying testing framework, JUnit or TestNG. As the reasons for choosing TestNG over JUnit for Integration Testing were already detailed in *Chapter 2 - Developer testing tools*, only quick mentions of JUnit will be described in this section.

The basics of using Spring Test are very straightforward - just extend AbstractTestNGSpringContextTests. This gives the benefits of all TestExecutionListener mentioned above, as well as a protected reference to the ApplicationContext referenced under the name applicationContext.

```java
public class SimpleSpringTest extends AbstractTestNGSpringContextTests {

    @BeforeMethod
    protected void setUp() throws Exception {
        MyClass myBean = applicationContext.getBean(MyClass.class);
        // Do something with myBean
    }
}
```

 # Do not call getBean()

Though Spring Test provides a reference to the application context, it is always better to inject dependencies than to call getBean() explicitly: whether in production or in testing code, this breaks Dependency Injection. The previous snippet should be replaced with the following:

```java
public class WrongSpringTest extends AbstractTestNGSpringContextTests {

    @Autowired
    private MyClass myBean;

    @BeforeMethod
    protected void setUp() throws Exception {
        // Do something with myBean
    }
}
```

At this point, the Spring framework does not know which configuration it should use
to initialize the application context - that's the role of the @ContextConfiguration
annotation. @ContextConfiguration can specify XML fragments through its locations
attribute and JavaConfig fragments - the preferred way, through its classes attribute.

```
@ContextConfiguration(classes = { MainConfig.class, AnotherConfig.class })
public class ConfigFragmentsSpringTest
        extends AbstractTestNGSpringContextTests {
    ...
}
```

7.3.2 Transaction management

As seen in section Database integration of *Chapter 5 - Infrastructure Resources
Integration*, some tests interact with databases (*e.g.* they execute SQL statements),
and need data to be persisted to the database after test execution. This require a
transaction, and specifically a commit.

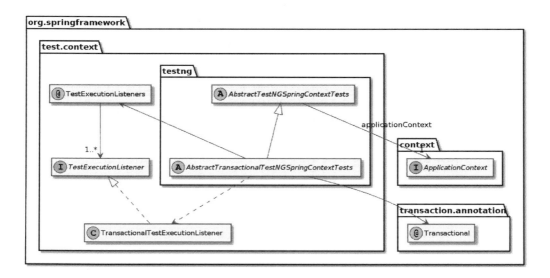

Fig. 7.8 - Spring Test TestNG class diagram

To achieve that, Spring Test provides the specialized AbstractTransactionalTestNGSpringContextTests class. It is akin to adding an additional TransactionalTestExecutionListener annotation as well as a @Transactional annotation on the test class. The previous diagram details this.

However, **by default, Spring will rollback the transaction** after each test execution. To commit transactions so that data gets persisted after test execution, one has to set the defaultRollback attribute of the @TransactionConfiguration annotation to false:

```
@ContextConfiguration
@TransactionConfiguration(defaultRollback = false)
public class NoRollbackSpringTest
    extends AbstractTransactionalTestNGSpringContextTests {
    ...
}
```

It is possible to override the global class behavior set with @TransactionConfiguration on each method with the @Rollback annotation:

```
@ContextConfiguration
@TransactionConfiguration(defaultRollback = false)
public class OverrideDefaultRollbackSpringTest
    extends AbstractTransactionalTestNGSpringContextTests {

    @Test
    @Rollback(true)
    public void transaction_will_be_rollbacked() { .. }

    @Test
    public void transaction_wont_be_rollbacked() { .. }
}
```

In order to manage transactions (START TRANSACTION, COMMIT and ROLLBACK), Spring will look in the application context for a transaction manager. By default, this is a PlatformTransactionManager bean named transactionManager. If more than one bean of this type exists in the context, or if it is named differently therein, it should be set explicitly with the `transactionManager` attribute of the `@TransactionConfiguration` annotation.

Spring adds two lifecycle phases to the standard lifecyle: before starting a transaction and after finishing one. Methods annotated with `@BeforeTransaction` and `@AfterTransaction` will be called during corresponding events.

7.4 Test doubles into the Spring context

As seen in *Chapter 1 - Foundations of Testin*, Integration Testing is about defining the System Under Test boundaries. Dependencies outside those boundaries have to be "test-doubled". Tools such as Mockito (seen in *Chapter 3 - Test-Friendly Design*) can be used to help in test-doubling those dependencies.

In order to achieve this, one has to craft a specific configuration fragment to override existing beans *e.g* create beans with exactly the same name as the *production* beans.

```
@Configuration
public class DoubleTestConfiguration {

    @Bean
    public CustomerRepository customerRepository() {
        return Mockito.mock(CustomerRepository.class);
    }
}
```

7.5 Case study: Spring Pet clinic part 1

In order to put in practice how to use the tools described above, let's use a "real" application, namely the famed Spring Pet clinic available at https://github.com/spring-projects/spring-petclinic/. This chapter will detail testing from the repository and services layers, while the next chapter will detail testing from the web layer.

For an overview of the application and the way it is designed, please look at this Speaker Deck presentation: https://speakerdeck.com/michaelisvy/spring-petclinic-sample-application. Take time to familiarize yourself with the design and the code before going any further.

7.5.1 Setup

Tests are going to be created in a dedicated Integration Testing project, so the original code is needed as a dependency. However, it seems the Spring Pet clinic is not deployed into any Maven repository. Some steps are necessary to go further:

1. Clone the Pet Clinic Github repo:

   ```
   git clone git@github.com:spring-projects/spring-petclinic.git
   ```

2. TheThe project was originally not meant to be used as a dependency, so a slight change is in order first: the original project is of packaging war to create a web application, but testing needs access to the sources, hence a JAR needs to be built.

   To do so, update the build/plugins section of the POM with the jar plugin:

Code 7.19 - Snippet to build both a JAR with the WAR

```
<artifactId>maven-jar-plugin</artifactId>
<version>2.5</version>
<executions>
    <execution>
        <goals>
            <goal>jar</goal>
        </goals>
    </execution>
</executions>
</plugin>
<plugin>
```

Then, in order to install the build JAR, update it with the `install` plugin:

Code 7.20 - Snippet to install both the JAR along with the WAR

```
<artifactId>maven-install-plugin</artifactId>
<version>2.5.1</version>
<executions>
    <execution>
        <phase>install</phase>
        <goals>
            <goal>install-file</goal>
        </goals>
        <configuration>
            <packaging>jar</packaging>
            <artifactId>${project.artifactId}</artifactId>
            <groupId>${project.groupId}</groupId>
            <version>${project.version}</version>
            <file>
${project.build.directory}/${project.artifactId}-${project.version}.jar
            </file>
        </configuration>
    </execution>
</executions>
</plugin>
            <plugin>
```

3. Install the dependency into the local Maven repository:

```
mvn install
```

Everything should be set at this point. And yes, there are already some tests in the code, but let's pretend there aren't and make our own.

The goal is to create integration tests at different levels: data access, business service and web controller.

7.5.2 Analysis of the current design

Before testing anything, a little analysis of the current design is in order.

- There are several XML configuration files, some of which use profiles. In particular, the `datasource-config.xml` file declares two datasources under the same `dataSource` bean name, one configured with a Tomcat pool, the other under the `javaee` profile configured with a JNDI lookup.
- The Tomcat pool reads its variable from the `data-access.properties` file. It is configured out-of-the-box to use an *in-memory* HSQL database.
- The `business-config.xml` file makes use of three profiles - one for each persistence framework implementation: JDBC, JPA and Spring Data JPA. Each profile declares a transaction manager and scans for repository classes as well as configures stuff specific to the framework (*e.g.* the JPA persistence unit). The configuration also scans for business service classes and manages transactions.

Notice that the Pet Clinic uses several approaches that were not discussed previously as well as sub-optimal design. This should be expected when dealing with an existing "real-life" application - they probably do not fit into the perfect scheme. For information, a non-exhaustive list of gaps includes:

- XML files are used for configuration instead of JavaConfig classes
- Implicit autowiring (and its corollary - component scanning) is used instead of explicit configuration
- There is one configuration file for both service and repository instead of one for each
- The data source configuration file mixes test and production beans
- The `business-config.xml` file imports the `datasource-config.xml` file so it is coupled to it, instead of letting the code (test or application) assemble the configuration

7.5.3 Repository layer

The Pet Clinic offers three different persistence strategies over the database: Spring Data JPA, raw JPA and JDBC. A real world application would probably not offer a choice in the persistence strategy. Let's choose one to test - this will be the JDBC implementation as it has the greatest potential for bugs. The `OwnerRepository` class will serve as a sample. It has three `public` methods that are to be tested:

- findById(int) finds an Owner by its primary key and either returns the found entity or throws an exception if no entity is found
- findByLastName(String) returns all Owners that match the last name
- save(Owner) creates **or** updates an Owner instance

> In a real-world application, testing those methods would probably be overkill, but they make a nice example in the context of a book.

Here is the proposed test class, the description follows:

Code 7.21 - Sample Pet Clinic repository test class

```java
1   import org.springframework.beans.factory.annotation.Autowired;
2   import org.springframework.orm.ObjectRetrievalFailureException;
3   import org.springframework.samples.petclinic.model.Owner;
4   import org.springframework.samples.petclinic.repository.OwnerRepository;
5   import org.springframework.test.context.*;
6   import org.springframework.test.context.testng.*;
7   import org.springframework.test.context.transaction.TransactionConfiguration;
8   import org.testng.Assert;
9   import org.testng.annotations.Test;
10
11  import java.util.Collection;
12
13  import static org.testng.Assert.*;
14
15  @ContextConfiguration("classpath:spring/business-config.xml")
16  @ActiveProfiles("jdbc")
17  @TransactionConfiguration(defaultRollback = false)
18  public class JdbcOwnerRepositoryImplIT
19          extends AbstractTransactionalTestNGSpringContextTests {
20
21      @Autowired
22      private OwnerRepository ownerRepository;
23
```

```java
24        private int createdOwnerId;
25
26      @Test
27      public void should_create_owner() {
28          Owner owner = new Owner();
29          owner.setFirstName("John");
30          owner.setLastName("Doe");
31          ownerRepository.save(owner);
32          createdOwnerId = owner.getId();
33          assertNotNull(createdOwnerId);
34      }
35
36      @Test(dependsOnMethods = "should_create_owner")
37      public void should_find_owner_by_id() {
38          Owner john = ownerRepository.findById(createdOwnerId);
39          assertNotNull(john);
40          assertEquals(john.getFirstName(), "John");
41      }
42
43      @Test(expectedExceptions = ObjectRetrievalFailureException.class)
44      public void should_throw_exception_if_no_owner_with_id_exists() {
45          ownerRepository.findById(-1);
46      }
47
48      @Test(dependsOnMethods = "should_create_owner")
49      public void should_find_owner_by_last_name() {
50          Collection<Owner> owners = ownerRepository.findByLastName("Doe");
51          assertNotNull(owners);
52          assertFalse(owners.isEmpty());
53          assertEquals(owners.size(), 1);
54          Owner john = owners.iterator().next();
55          assertEquals(john.getFirstName(), "John");
56      }
57
58      @Test(dependsOnMethods = "should_find_owner_by_id")
59      public void should_update_owner() {
60          Owner john = ownerRepository.findById(createdOwnerId);
61          john.setFirstName("John1");
```

```
62        ownerRepository.save(john);
63        Owner john1 = ownerRepository.findById(john.getId());
64        assertEquals(john1.getFirstName(), "John1");
65    }
66 }
```

Line 15

This tells the Spring framework which configuration fragments should be loaded. Here, the file is business-config.xml, which in turn imports the datasource-config.xml file.

Line 16

The implementation under test is the JDBC one, so the configured profile needs to be set to jdbc.

Line 17

This is an integration test, not a unit test. **Transactions must be committed** for two possible reasons:

- Diagnostics: check the database state after tests have failed. This is obviously not the case here as the database runs in memory.
- IntegrationTesting: methods might (and will, see below) depend on one another so that an owner written in a method can be reused with the same state in other methods.

To do so, the @TransactionConfiguration annotation is used with the defaultRollback value set to false.

Lines 18-19

As with any other integration test, this one must inherit from AbstractTestNGSpringContextTests to load the context and inject the required beans. In this case, the inherited class must be AbstractTransactionalTestNGSpringContextTests to handle transactions.

Lines 21-22

Simply inject the instance under test

Line 24

An attribute to store the ID of the created entity in method should_create_-
owner(), to be reused in find() methods

Lines 26-34

Tests the INSERT part of the save() method by asserting that a newly instantiated owner has had an set ID after it has been saved. The ID is stored to be
reused in other methods.

Lines 36-41

Tests the standard behavior of the findById() method by searching for the
previously created owner, using the stored ID. This test has been configured to
run after the save() method.

Lines 43-46

Tests the exceptional behavior of the findById() method. There is nothing
specific to Integration Testing - except that it uses a database.

Lines 48-56

Tests the standard behavior of the findByLastName() method by searching for
the previously created owner. It uses the ID created during save().

Lines 58-65

Tests the UPDATE part of the save() method by loading the owner, modifying
it, saving it, then loading it again.

7.5.4 Service layer

The Pet Clinic service layer is extremely thin as it is a CRUD application. Basically, it
is just a single ClinicServiceImpl class serving as an entry-point for controllers to
repositories. Two features can still be tested: transactions and cache. Testing the cache
is easy enough - the first service call should interact with the underlying repository,
while the second and subsequent ones should not as the cache has been filled. As the
cache also serves as a good example for mixing standard beans and test doubles, let's
test cache configuration.

As seen in section Test doubles into the Spring context above, inserting test doubles
into the Spring context requires creating a dedicated configuration fragment.

Spring Test @ContextConfiguration annotation cannot be configured
with both XML and JavaConfig fragments. Therefore as Pet Clinic is
configured using XML, the fragment for doubles must also (unfortunately)
be in XML format. Fortunately, Spring provides a way to call static
methods using the factory-method attribute.

Here is the XML fragment for creating a mock:

Code 7.22 - Mock Spring configuration

```xml
1   <?xml version="1.0" encoding="UTF-8"?>
2   <beans...>
3       <bean id="jdbcVetRepositoryImpl" class="org.mockito.Mockito"
4           factory-method="mock">
5           <constructor-arg value="o.s.s.petclinic.repository.VetRepository" />
6       </bean>
7   </beans>
```

The next step is of course the test class itself:

Code 7.23 - Testing cache configuration

```java
1   import org.springframework.beans.factory.annotation.Autowired;
2   import org.springframework.samples.petclinic.model.Vet;
3   import org.springframework.samples.petclinic.repository.VetRepository;
4   import org.springframework.samples.petclinic.service.ClinicService;
5   import org.springframework.test.context.ActiveProfiles;
6   import org.springframework.test.context.ContextConfiguration;
7   import org.springframework.test.context.testng.*;
8   import org.testng.annotations.BeforeMethod;
9   import org.testng.annotations.Test;
10
11  import java.util.*;
12
13  import static org.mockito.Mockito.*;
14  import static org.testng.Assert.*;
15
```

```
16   @ContextConfiguration({
17           "classpath:cache-test-config.xml",
18           "classpath:spring/tools-config.xml",
19           "classpath:spring/business-config.xml"
20   })
21   @ActiveProfiles("jdbc")
22   public class ClinicServiceIT
23           extends AbstractTransactionalTestNGSpringContextTests {
24
25       @Autowired
26       private ClinicService clinicService;
27
28       @Autowired
29       private VetRepository vetRepository;
30
31       @BeforeMethod
32       protected void setUp() {
33           Collection<Vet> vets = Arrays.asList(new Vet(), new Vet());
34           when(vetRepository.findAll()).thenReturn(vets);
35       }
36
37       @Test
38       public void should_use_cache_after_first_call() {
39           clinicService.findVets();
40           verify(vetRepository).findAll();
41           Collection<Vet> vets = clinicService.findVets();
42           verifyZeroInteractions(vetRepository);
43           assertNotNull(vets);
44           assertFalse(vets.isEmpty());
45           assertEquals(2, vets.size());
46       }
47   }
```

Lines 16-20

As with the repository layer test, the test configuration is achieved via annotations. The only difference is two additional XML configuration fragments: obviously, the previously created one for the mock and the one for caching -

tools-config.xml. Also notice there is no need to manage transactions, so the @TransactionConfiguration annotation is not necessary.

Lines 28-35

The injected vetRepository is set up. As it is a mock, Mockito is used to graft the behavior to provide dummy vets.

Lines 37-46

Those lines are the test's "meat". The first verify() verifies there has been a single call from the service to the repository, to check the latter has been called. The second one verifies there has been none, ensuring the vets are returned from the cache.

7.6 Summary

This chapter detailed several techniques to allow for Integration Testing with the Spring framework. The most important is to separate beans into two different groups: beans that will be used in both production and testing contexts, and beans that will be different depending on the context. Then, put these beans depending on their nature in different configuration fragments. Fragment management can be quite complex with JavaConfig, but in this regard, profiles are a convenient way to ease it.

Configuration parameterization has been described as an alternative or an improvement to configuration fragments. It includes .properties files and ways to read them through the Spring framework in the light of Integration Testing.

An important asset of the Spring framework is the module called Spring Test. It provides complete integration with JUnit and TestNG. Integration with the latter has been fully described, including how to get a reference on the application context, how to inject specific beans into tests and how to manage transactions in a test context.

To finish the chapter, a case study dedicated to the classic Pet Clinic has been applied to the repository and service layers, using tools and techniques found in the current and previous chapters.

The next chapter will show how to go further with Integration Testing with Spring applications and describe specifics for Spring web applications. It will contains the second part of the case study, entirely devoted to the web layer.

8. Spring Web MVC testing

Spring is not only one of the earliest Dependency Injection frameworks in Java, it also builds upon its Dependency Injection core to provide an extremely powerful and productive way to develop web applications.

As the previous chapter described how to enable Integration Testing for Spring applications, this chapter is dedicated to doing the same for Spring **web** applications. This includes:

- Creating Spring context hierarchies that mimic those created by Spring for web applications
- Testing Spring webapps with URLs as entry points

The chapter will conclud with the second (and final) part of the case-study of Spring Pet Clinic and put to use what was covered in the first part of the chapter.

8.1 Context hierarchies

The previous chapter showed how to test Spring applications that use a single context. However, some Spring applications - and that includes **web** applications, rely on contexts that are part of a context hierarchy. Such hierarchies are organized in one- parent-to-many-children relationships. Child contexts can access their parent's context while the opposite is not true.

To simulate this relationship in a testing context, Spring Test provides the @ContextHierarchy annotation. @ContextHierarchy accepts a sequential list of @ContextConfiguration: each context is the direct parent of the context next to him in the sequence. @ContextHierarchy should be set on the test class.

```
@ContextHierarchy({
    @ContextConfiguration(classes = MainConfig.class),
    @ContextConfiguration(classes = AnotherConfig.class)
})
public class ContextHierarchySpringTest
    extends AbstractTestNGSpringContextTests {
    ...
}
```

The snippet above creates two contexts, one hydrated from the MainConfig class and one from the AnotherConfig class. It also sets the first context as the parent and the second one as the child.

8.1.1 Web context hierarchies

Web applications can be developed with the Spring framework thanks to its MVC (*Model-View-Controller*) module. While Spring creates a standard context, Spring MVC creates a dedicated web context and attaches it to the former as a child.

In order for Spring Test to create a WebApplicationContext instead of a simple ApplicationContext, it provides the @WebAppConfiguration annotation to set on the test class:

```
@WebAppConfiguration
@ContextHierarchy({
    @ContextConfiguration(classes = MainConfig.class),
    @ContextConfiguration(classes = WebConfig.class)
})
public class SpringWebApplicationTest
    extends AbstractTestNGSpringContextTests {
    ...
}
```

The previous test configuration ensures the following:

- A context will be created from the MainConfig configuration class

- A specialized web context will be created from the `WebConfig` configuration class
- The later will be attached to the former as its child
- `applicationContext` will be of *runtime* type `WebApplicationContext`. This means **it must be cast** to use any method coming from the subclass

8.2 Testing Spring MVC applications

Previously, whatever the scope of the System Under Test, it has been limited solely to raw code. However, modern applications are mostly **web applications**, accessible through the HTTP protocol. Armed only with the knowledge from previous chapters, testing a webapp would mean testing using controller methods as entry points. This would only be shallow integration, as Spring MVC provides tons of features that come from outside the controller's scope, like mapping URLs to controllers, internationalization, error handling, interceptors, etc.

As Integration Testing increases the confidence in application code, further increasing this confidence requires testing at a much higher level of abstraction. This level is HTTP and translates into sending crafted HTTP requests and checking the associated HTTP responses. There are two different ways to achieve this:

- One approach is to look at applications from the Graphical User Interface viewpoint e.g. click on this button and check this field value. The Selenium (http://www.seleniumhq.org/) framework adopts this approach.
- The other point of view is to look at the application from the HTTP protocol itself. The HTMLUnit (http://htmlunit.sourceforge.net/) frameworks uses this strategy.

Both ways work and have the advantage of not being tailored to the Java language. On the downside, they are both fragile: locating GUI components is done through the Document Object Model which is ever-changing during the development of an application. Crafting HTTP requests is easy enough, but checking the result is usually achieved by looking at the generated HTML and this brings us back to the previous problem. In both cases, this requires a definite strategy to bring a positive Return Over Investment. Between GUI, HTTP and methods, there is a definite place for something in-between tailored for Spring web applications. This is exactly what Spring Test provides, with a large part dedicated to Spring MVC.

At the heart of the MVC testing framework lies the MockMvc class. To create a MockMvc instance, use either of the static method of the MockMvcBuilders class:

- For testing applications simple standalone controllers, use standaloneSetup(Object...) with parameters being the controller classes
- For testing more complex use cases - which is nearly the case, use webAppContextSetup(WebApplicationContext)

Fig. 8.1 - How to get a MockMvc instance

 Spring Boot

Java EE applications are meant to run in an application server. The original goal of the Spring framework was to ease Java EE development so that they could run in a simple Servlet/JSP container, such as Apache Tomcat or Jetty. In many cases, to make resource management easier, only a single application is deployed to a container. Spring Boot (http://projects.spring.io/spring-boot/) is a new project by Spring that goes a step further to run **standalone** with no deployment necessary *i.e.* through an embedded servlet container.

The MockMvc class itself is relatively small, it only provides a perform() method. It is however at the center of a complete class hierarchy, organized as follows:

1. As their name implies, request builders are responsible for creating Fake HTTP requests
2. Result handlers execute an action
3. Result matchers check the result of the execution and test against an expectation

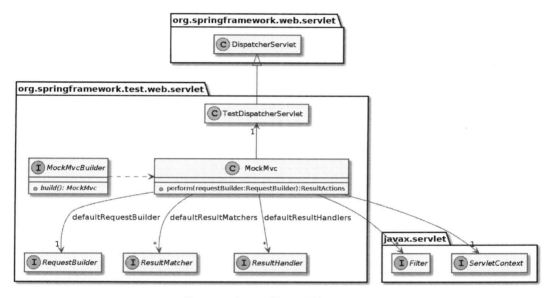

Fig. 8.2 - Spring Test MVC overview

8.2.1 Request builder

A request builder is used to build Fake request objects. `RequestBuilder` is a simple interface offering a single `buildRequest(ServletContext)` that returns a `MockHttpServletRequest` object.

It implements the Builder (http://en.wikipedia.org/wiki/Builder_pattern) pattern through the `MockHttpServletRequestBuilder`. Instances of the latter can be obtained through the `MockMvcRequestBuilders` factory (notice the plural in the class name). There is one factory method for each HTTP method, named after the method, but in lower case: `get()`, `put()`, `post()`, `options()`, `patch()` and `delete()`. All methods are available in two different overloaded flavors:

- One takes a single URI parameter
- The other one accepts a String for an URI template and varargs Object for variables. The URI template (*e.g.* get("/customer/{customerId}")) will be resolved by the testing framework. For a refresher on Spring MVC URI templates, please look at the online documentation: http://docs.spring.io/spring/docs/current/spring-framework-reference/html/mvc.html#mvc-ann-requestmapping-uri-templates.

 There is also one generic MockMvcRequestBuilders.request() method that takes an extra HttpMethod to allow for custom HTTP methods.

MockHttpServletRequestBuilder offers a lot of configuration features for the resulting Fake request in the form of a fluent API. There are two types of configuration methods:

- Those related to the HTTP protocol itself
- Those related to the Java EE API

Table 8.1 - MockHttpServletRequestBuilder HTTP configuration method summary

Method	Parameter(s)	Description
accept	MediaType... String...	Sets HTTP Accept headers
characterEncoding	String	Sets the charset part of the HTTP Content-Type header
content	byte[] String	Sets the request content
contentType	MediaType	Sets the HTTP Content-Type header
header	String, String... HttpHeaders	Sets any HTTP header

Java EE related setters are the opposite of standard Java EE API getters.

Table 8.2 - MockHttpServletRequestBuilder Java EE configuration method summary

Method	Parameter(s)	Description
cookie	Cookie...	Sets cookies
locale	Locale	Sets the locale
param	String, String...	Sets a parameter on the query string
principal	Principal	Sets the Principal
requestAttr	String, Object	Sets a request attribute
sessionAttr	String, Object	Sets a session attribute
sessionAttrs	Map<String, Object>	Sets multiple session attributes at once
secure	boolean	If true, sets the protocol as secure such as HTTPS
servletPath	String	Sets the servlet path
session	MockHttpSession	Sets a Fake HTTP session

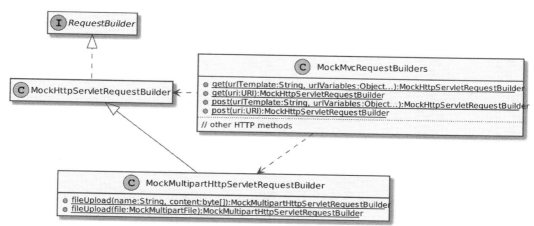

Fig. 8.3 - Request Builder class hierarchy

Using these methods makes it really easy to craft the desired Fake request, to be used as an input for testing purpose.

Here is a sample of such code:

Code 8.1 - Mock MVC request builder sample

```
1   MockHttpServletRequestBuilder builder = get("/customer/{id}", 1234L)
2                       .accept("text/html")
3                       .param("lang", "en")
4                       .secure(true);
5   MockHttpServletRequest request = builder.buildRequest(servletContext);
6                   assertEquals(request.isSecure(), true);
```

The previous Fake request will emulate the following request:

```
GET /customer/1234?lang=en HTTP/1.1
Accept: text/html
```

However, the main usage of a request builder is not to create a MockHttpServletRequest instance (though it certainly can), but to pass the RequestBuilder object to the perfom() method of a MockMvc instance.

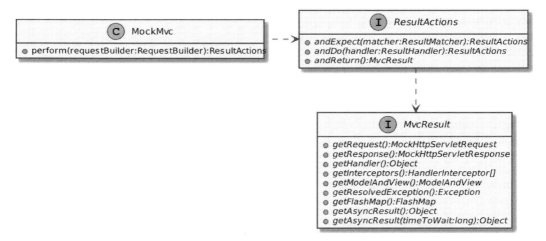

Fig. 8.4 - Request builder usage

The return value of perfom() is a ResultActions instance: through this instance, it is possible to chain calls through a pipeline of ResultMatcher and ResultHandler.

8.2.2 Result handler

A request handler is used to execute actions on a `ResultActions` instance. Spring provides a handler out-of-the-box to print an `MvcResult`'s complete details to the standard output.

It can be used without knowing any of the details:

Code 8.2 - Result handler usage example

```
1  DefaultMockMvcBuilder mockMvcBuilder =
2          webAppContextSetup((WebApplicationContext) applicationContext);
3  MockMvc mockMvc = mockMvcBuilder.build();
4  MockHttpServletRequestBuilder getCustomer = get("/customer/{id}", 1234L)
5          .accept("text/html")
6          .param("lang", "en")
7          .secure(true);
8  mockMvc.perform(getCustomer).andDo(print());
```

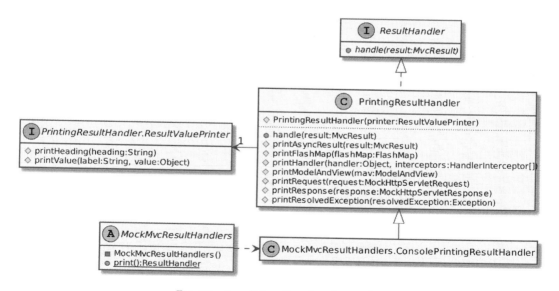

Fig. 8.5 - Result handler class hierarchy

Writing to `System.out` should be avoided in production applications, but is acceptable in test code. Should one need to choose another option instead, the above diagram displays the result handler class hierarchy.

To use a specific logging framework, the steps are:

- Provide one's own implementation of `ResultValuePrinter` *e.g.*
  `Slf4JResultValuePrinter`
- Inherit from `PrintingResultHandler` *e.g.* `Slf4JPrintingResultHandler`
- Instantiate the latter and pass an instance of the former as a parameter

```
PrintingResultHandler resultHandler =
    new Slf4JPrintingResultHandler(new Slf4JResultValuePrinter());
```

8.2.3 Result matcher

A result matcher is a Spring MVC kind of assertion for a result. The `MockMvcResultMatchers` class is an entry point that returns either:

- `ResultMatcher` instances
- Objects dedicated to provide different types of `ResultMatcher`. Think of them as classes that offer a way to return tightly-grouped matchers.

Result matchers available directly at the `MockMvcResultMatchers` via static methods are:

Static method	Checks the result is a...
`forwardedUrl(expectedUrl:String)`	Forward to the exact given URL
`forwardedUrlPattern(urlPattern:String)`	Forward and matches the URL regexp
`jsonPath(expression:String, matcher:Matcher<T>)`	JSON payload. The first argument is a JSONPath (http://goessner.net/articles/JsonPath/), the second is a Hamcrest (http://hamcrest.org/JavaHamcrest/) matcher.
`redirectedUrl(expectedUrl:String)`	Redirect to the exact given URL
`redirectedUrlPattern(expectedUrl:String`	Redirect and matches the URL regexp

Other static methods returning a grouping object are:

Static method	Type	Checks about result's...
content()	ContentResultMatchers	Content
cookie()	CookieResultMatchers	Cookies
flash()	FlashAttributeResultMatchers	Flash attributes
handler()	HandlerResultMatchers	Handling controller
model()	ModelResultMatchers	Underlying model
request()	RequestResultMatchers	Request itself
status()	StatusResultMatchers	HTTP code
view()	ViewResultMatchers	Underlying view

 Note there also is a static `xpath(expression:String, namespaces:Map<String, String, args:Object...)` method returning an XpathResultMatchers. As its name implies, it matches responses against an XPath expression. This fine-grained check might be useful in very limited use-cases, but in general just makes the integration test too fragile.

8.3 Case study: Spring Pet Clinic part 2

The previous chapter saw the testing of both the repository and service layers - or more accurately, a sample of them. Time to apply the knowledge gained from the sections above to the web layer.

 ## To mock or not to mock?

The first question is whether to mock (or fake) some of the lower layer. In this case, the Pet Clinic comes with an in-memory database, so we expect reasonably fast response times: there is no need to use any test double.

8.3.1 Testing the pet controller

The `PetController` is a good candidate for Integration Testing, as it offers different methods mapped to HTTP entry points. The source code can be found online in Spring's Github project: https://github.com/spring-projects/spring-petclinic/blob/master/src/main/java/org/springframework/samples/petclinic/web/PetController.java.

The easiest method to test is `initCreationForm(int, Map<String, Object>)`, that forwards to the form to create a new pet. Calling this method does a couple of things that might be worth testing:

- It forwards to the `pets/createOrUpdatePetForm` view
- It reads `Pet` from the database and stores it under the `pet` key in the model
- It reads all `PetType` from the database and stores the collection under the `types` key in the model

  Note that this could **not** be tested using "standard" Java ways, as reading is done in the `populatePetTypes()` method and called automatically by Spring MVC because of the `@ModelAttribute` annotation on the later method.

A proposed test to check the previous items looks like the following:

Code 8.3 - Pet creation form initialization IT proposal

```
1   import org.springframework.test.context.*;
2   import o.s.test.context.testng.AbstractTestNGSpringContextTests;
3   import org.springframework.test.context.web.WebAppConfiguration;
4   import org.springframework.test.web.servlet.MockMvc;
5   import o.s.test.web.servlet.request.MockHttpServletRequestBuilder;
6   import org.springframework.test.web.servlet.setup.MockMvcBuilders;
7   import org.springframework.web.context.WebApplicationContext;
8   import org.testng.annotations.Test;
9
10  import static o.s.test.web.servlet.request.MockMvcRequestBuilders.get;
11  import static o.s.test.web.servlet.result.MockMvcResultMatchers.*;
12
13
14  @WebAppConfiguration
```

```
15   @ContextHierarchy({
16       @ContextConfiguration("classpath:spring/business-config.xml"),
17       @ContextConfiguration("classpath:spring/mvc-core-config.xml")
18   })
19   @ActiveProfiles("jdbc")
20   public class PetControllerIT extends AbstractTestNGSpringContextTests {
21
22       @Test
23       public void should_display_create_form() throws Exception {
24           WebApplicationContext wac =
25               (WebApplicationContext) applicationContext;
26           MockMvc mvc = MockMvcBuilders.webAppContextSetup(wac).build();
27           MockHttpServletRequestBuilder newPet =
28               get("/owners/{ownerId}/pets/new", 1);
29           mvc.perform(newPet).andExpect(view()
30               .name("pets/createOrUpdatePetForm"))
31               .andExpect(model().attributeExists("pet"))
32               .andExpect(model().attributeExists("types"));
33       }
34   }
```

This code tests the previous facts: forwarding at line 28, storing the pet in the model at line 29 and the types at line 30.

 ## What exactly should I test?

Checking the other results the method achieves *e.g.* set the pet's owner, is definitely an option. However this may make the test too fragile... or not. This is exactly the kind of decision that awaits software engineers who want to increase their application's quality with integration tests.

Once initialization of the creation form has been tested, it is time to test the creation itself handled by the processCreationForm(Pet, BindingResult, SessionStatus) method. Results of the previous initCreationForm() method were only pure Spring and could be asserted as such. However, the present method also insert a row in the database and this is a pretty important output, so that has to be asserted too. This check could be achieved through DBUnit as seen in *Chapter 5 - Data management with DBUnit* but it would be too much of a hassle as an existing Repository can be used instead, and with much less hassle.

This leads to the following test:

Code 8.4 - Pet creation IT proposal

```
1   import org.joda.time.DateTime;
2   import org.springframework.beans.factory.annotation.Autowired;
3   import org.springframework.samples.petclinic.model.*;
4   import org.springframework.samples.petclinic.repository.*;
5   import org.springframework.test.context.*;
6   import o.s.test.context.testng.AbstractTestNGSpringContextTests;
7   import org.springframework.test.context.web.WebAppConfiguration;
8   import org.springframework.test.web.servlet.MockMvc;
9   import o.s.test.web.servlet.request.MockHttpServletRequestBuilder;
10  import org.springframework.test.web.servlet.setup.MockMvcBuilders;
11  import org.springframework.web.context.WebApplicationContext;
12  import org.testng.annotations.*;
13
14  import static o.s.test.web.servlet.request.MockMvcRequestBuilders.post;
15  import static o.s.test.web.servlet.result.MockMvcResultMatchers.*;
16  import static org.testng.Assert.assertEquals;
17
18
19  @WebAppConfiguration
20  @ContextHierarchy({
21      @ContextConfiguration("classpath:spring/business-config.xml"),
22      @ContextConfiguration("classpath:spring/mvc-core-config.xml")
23  })
24  @ActiveProfiles("jdbc")
25  public class PetControllerIT extends AbstractTestNGSpringContextTests {
26
27      @Autowired
28      private PetRepository petRepository;
29
30      @Autowired
31      private OwnerRepository ownerRepository;
```

```
32
33      private Owner george;
34      private PetType cat;
35      private Pet johnDoe;
36
37      @BeforeMethod
38      protected void setUp() {
39          george = new Owner();
40          george.setId(1);
41          cat = new PetType();
42          cat.setId(1);
43          johnDoe = new Pet();
44          johnDoe.setName("John Doe");
45          johnDoe.setBirthDate(new DateTime());
46          johnDoe.setType(cat);
47          george.addPet(johnDoe);
48      }
49
50      @Test
51      public void should_create_new_pet() throws Exception {
52          WebApplicationContext wac =
53              (WebApplicationContext) applicationContext;
54          MockMvc mvc = MockMvcBuilders.webAppContextSetup(wac).build();
55          MockHttpServletRequestBuilder newPet =
56              post("/owners/{ownerId}/pets/new", george.getId())
57              .sessionAttr("pet", johnDoe);
58          mvc.perform(newPet).andExpect(
59              redirectedUrl("/owners/" + george.getId()))
60              .andExpect(model().attributeExists("types"));
61          Pet actualPet = petRepository.findById(14);
62          assertEquals(actualPet.getName(), johnDoe.getName());
63          assertEquals(actualPet.getType().getId(), johnDoe.getType().getId());
64          assertEquals(actualPet.getOwner().getId(),
65                      johnDoe.getOwner().getId());
66      }
67  }
```

Lines 37-48

The `Pet` entity created from the controller needs to be set up, as well as its dependent objects, an `Owner` and a `PetType`. Note that the owner and the type just need to have an id set. To set the right id, just peek at the SQL script named `populateDB.sql` and notice `types` id 1 is `'cat'` and `owners` id 1 is `'george'`. Though not strictly necessary, those values make the test more readable.

Lines 54-60

This snippet is similar to the previous test. Slight differences include:

- Using a `post()` instead of a `get()`
- Expecting a redirect to a view instead of a forward to it

The real difference comes from line 57 proper: the `Pet` instance created during set up is stored in the session scope to make it available to the controller.

Line 61

This line uses the autowired repository to load the `Pet` instance. The id of the `Pet` to be found is infered by adding 1 to the maximum value of the id of the pet inserted in the `populateDB.sql` script.

Lines 62-65

The `Pet` class does not override the `equals(Object)` method, thus each individual field has to be checked. Note that the `birthDate` field cannot be asserted as is: the `birth_date` database column is of type `DATE` which removes lower field information.

8.4 Summary

This chapter explained how to use context hierarchies for testing, thanks to the `@ContextHierarchy` annotation and how make them web application context with the `@WebAppConfiguration` annotation.

The rest of the chapter described the part of Spring Test aimed at the Spring MVC framework. At the heart of the test framework lies the `MockMvc` class, it can be obtained through the `MockMvcBuilders.webAppContextSetup()` static method. At this point, Spring Test offers 3 different pluggable classes:

- RequestBuilder to build the test request. It can be configured with parameters, attributes, etc.
- ResultHandler to do something with the result. The only provided implementation just prints out the result to the console, but one can provide other useful implementations.
- ResultMatcher to verify the result. Many checks are provided out-of-the-box: related to headers, views, redirects, forwards, model, etc.

This chapter concludes the description of testing Spring applications. The next chapter will cover the Java EE world and relevant tools.

9. Java EE testing

Last but not least, this chapter is dedicated to testing Java EE applications. Java EE (formerly J2EE) has been the standard promoted by Sun - then Oracle - to develop enterprise applications.

Java EE applications have always been hard to test. Previously (until v3.0), Enterprise Java Beans were bound to the container so that they were impossible to Unit Test. Context and Dependency Injection (http://cdi-spec.org/), also known as CDI or JSR-299, brought an end to this. Now, any class - not only EJB - can be injected, and thus be the target of Unit Testing. However, Integration Testing still has not breached the Java EE walls, partly because injection is implicit: every class available is a candidate for injection. This makes it impossible to define a System Under Test that is not the complete system.

Moreover, Java EE comes with the promise of applications running in the exact same way on every compliant server. It is the author's experience that this is not the case, especially for some parts of the Java EE specifications. Whereas the Web part is very well defined, EJB specifications leave some space to the application server implementation. For applications that always run on the same server, it is acceptable to bend to its quirks, but for products that aim to be deployed on any server, this is a great show stopper.

This chapter will cover Arquillian and Shrinkwrap, Open Source free tools to resolve these problems in an elegant way.

9.1 Shrinkwrap

Dependency Injection in the Java EE world is based on autowiring (and the `@Inject` annotation). With explicit Dependency Injection, the definition of a System Under Test is done by creating dedicated configuration to pick the required beans. With Java EE autowiring, all classes on the classpath are candidates for autowiring.

Therefore, creating a package that has only the required classes is the only way to define a SUT that is not the entire application. This is the main objective of Shrinkwrap.

9.1.1 Using Shrinkwrap

Shrinkwrap is architected along 3 modules: the Application Programmer Interface (API), the Service Provider Interface (SPI) and the implementation. The first is of course a compile-time dependency while the other twos are runtime dependencies for standard usage.

The good news is that Shrinkwrap provides a Maven artifact of type POM that is already configured for such usage. Just add the following snippet to the POM:

Code 9.1 - Shrinkwrap Maven dependency configuration

```
<!-- Other dependencies -->
<dependency>
    <groupId>org.jboss.shrinkwrap</groupId>
    <artifactId>shrinkwrap-depchain</artifactId>
    <version>1.2.2</version>
    <type>pom</type>
    <scope>test</scope>
</dependency>
</dependencies>
</project>
```

9.1.2 Shrinkwrap's model

Shrinkwrap's model revolves around the following concepts:

- Archive: a Java EE artifact (JAR, WAR, etc.)
- Node: an entry in an archive
- ArchivePath: the location of a node inside an archive
- Asset: byte-content (either class or resource) associated with a node

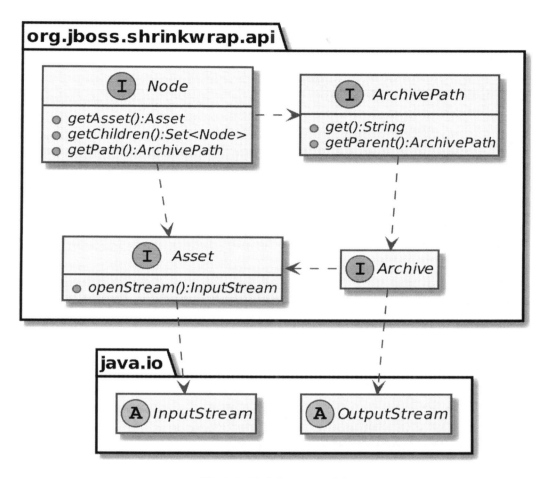

Fig. 9.1 - Shrinkwrap model

There is a child interface of `Archive` for each Java EE artifact: `JavaArchive` for JAR, `WebArchive` for WAR, `ResourceAdaptorArchive` for RAR and `EnterpriseArchive` for EAR.

9.1.3 Creating archives

The entry point for creating such an artifact is easy, using the `Shrinkwrap.create(Class<T>, String)` static method, where:

- The T generics should be a subtype of Archive (though it is not specified as such)
- The String is the artifact's name. The default, if not specified, is a random UUID plus the artifact's extension.

Code 9.2 - Creating archives with Shrinkwrap

```
JavaArchive myJar = ShrinkWrap.create(JavaArchive.class, "myJar.jar");
WebArchive myWar  = ShrinkWrap.create(WebArchive.class,  "myWar.war");
```

9.1.4 Adding assets to archives

Actually, the previous snippets do create artifacts - but empty ones: not a very interesting outcome. Shrinkwrap fortunately allows us to stuff resources into artifacts. As seen from the model above, this translates into getting Assets and putting them under an ArchivePath into the to-be-created Archive.

Available asset types to put in archives are the following:

Table 9.1 - Available asset types

Asset type	Description
ClassAsset	Resources on the classpath
ByteArrayAsset	Byte arrays and input streams
FileAsset	Files
StringAsset	Simple strings
ClassLoaderAsset	Resources located by another classloader
ArchiveAsset	References to other archives Useful for putting JARs in WARs, and WARs in EARs, etc.
EmptyAsset	Empty content Useful for putting empty resources in the archive

Other asset types

If none of the above assets match your requirements, remember that Asset is an interface and create the desired implementation.

There are several ways to add assets to an archive. The most straightforward way is to instantiate an asset's concrete implementation and add it to the archive under the desired location archive. This is done with the help of the Archive.add(Asset, String) method, where the second parameter represents the path in the archive.

Code 9.3 - Putting assets in archives

```
myJar.add(new ClassAsset(my.own.Clazz.class), "my/own/Clazz");
myWar.add(new FileAsset(
    new File("javaee/src/test/resources/web.xml")), "WEB-INF/web.xml");
```

Shrinkwrap allows you to check the structure of the created archives through the overloaded Archive.toString(boolean) method, with the boolean value true.

Code 9.4 - Printing archive's structures

```
System.out.println(myJar.toString(true));
System.out.println(myWar.toString(true));
```

This prints the following output:

```
myJar.jar:
/my/
/my/own/
/my/own/Clazz
myWar.war:
/WEB-INF/
/WEB-INF/web.xml
```

The previously described way to add assets to archives has two glitches:

1. It requires knowing how to instantiate each type of asset
2. Declaring the path for a file makes sense, declaring the path for a class is redundant

Therefore, Shrinkwrap adds methods to each archive subtype dedicated to each asset relevant to the archive subtype. This is implemented through a hierachy of container interfaces, every interface having a dedicated responsibility.

9.1.4.1 Adding assets to Java archives

The hierarchy for `JavaArchive` is as follows:

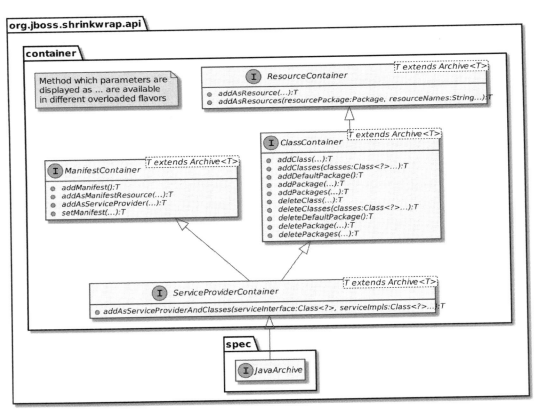

Fig. 9.2 - Java archive class hierarchy

As seen from the above diagram, Java archives have dedicated methods to add some assets: generic resources, manifests, classes and packages. Moreover, methods return the current instance so that it offers a fluent API through chained method calls.

 ## Overloaded add methods

Most add methods accept different parameter types: String references for classpath-relative locations in the source project, but other types are available such as File, URL or Asset.

As an example, let's create a Java archive from an existing project.

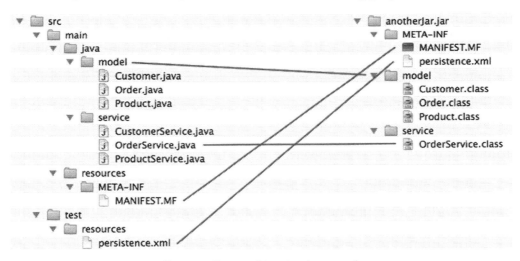

Fig. 9.3 - Java archive simple example

The structure on the left shows the available assets, while the structure on the right shows the desired output. Lines map from the asset's original location to the output's target location. Here is a code proposal to achieve that:

Code 9.5 - Creating a more complex Java archive

```
1    JavaArchive jar = ShrinkWrap.create(JavaArchive.class, "anotherJar.jar")
2                    .addClass(OrderService.class)
3                    .addPackage(Order.class.getPackage())
4                    .addAsResource("persistence.xml", "META-INF/persistence.xml")
5                    .setManifest("META-INF/MANIFEST.MF");
```

Line 2

> The OrderService class is needed. That's easy enough thanks to the JavaArchive.addClass(Class<?>) method. It uses the target class as the parameter.

Line 3

> Shrinkwrap offers the JavaArchive.addPackage(Package) method to add all classes from a specific package, *e.g.* all classes from the model package. To get a reference to the Package object, get a reference to the Class and call the Class.getPackage() method.

Line 4

> A specially-configured persistence.xml file is required. It is available from the src/test/resources folder and can be copied to the archive thanks to the JavaArchive.addAsResource(String, String). The first parameter is the classpath location of the source, the second the classpath location of the target in the archive.

Line 5

> The last step is to set the manifest with the help of the JavaArchive.setManifest(String) method, which uses the file located in src/main/resources.

9.1.4.2 Adding assets to Web archives

Along with Java archives, Web archives - also known as WARs - are another commonly-required package type.

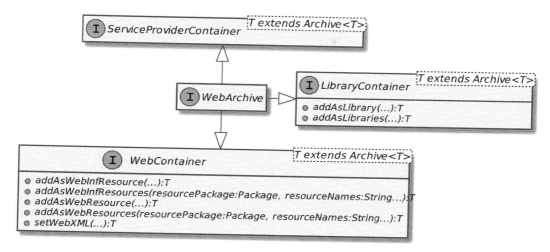

Fig. 9.4 - Web archive class hierarchy

Besides adding classes, `WebArchive` adds several methods to add assets specific to WARs:

- Resources put in the document root of the WAR, fully accessible when deployed
- Resources put in the `WEB-INF` directory of the WAR, protected from external access when deployed
- Web XML deployment descriptor, set to `WEB-INF/web.xml`
- JAR libraries put in the `WEB-INF/lib` directory

Let's do the same exercise for the WAR as previously for the JAR.

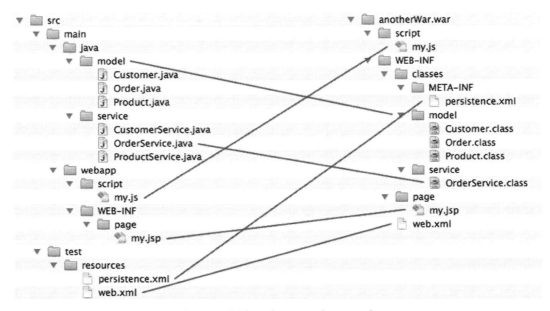

Fig. 9.5 - Web archive simple example

Code 9.6 - Creating a more complex Web archive

```
1   String srcMainWebapp = "src/main/webapp/";
2   WebArchive war = ShrinkWrap.create(WebArchive.class, "anotherWar.war")
3       .addClass(OrderService.class)
4       .addPackage(Order.class.getPackage())
5       .addAsWebInfResource(
6           "persistence.xml", "classes/META-INF/persistence.xml")
7       .addAsWebInfResource(
8           new File(srcMainWebapp, "WEB-INF/page/my.jsp"), "page/my.jsp")
9       .addAsWebResource(
10          new File(srcMainWebapp, "script/my.js"), "script/my.js")
11      .setWebXML("web.xml");
```

Lines 3-4

Classes are copied to the target Web archive using the same methods as for a Java archive.

Lines 5-6

In a WAR, the persistence.xml file needs to be copied to the

WEB-INF/classes/META-INF folder, as per the specifications. It is possible to do this thanks to the WebArchive.addAsWebInfResource(String, String) method, where the first parameter is the classpath location of the source, the second the WEB-INF-relative location of the target in the archive.

Lines 7-8

Pages are other web resources that need to be put into the WEB-INF WEB-INF of the target archive. The same method as in the previous point can be used, the difference being that the first parameter is not on the classpath and thus cannot be referenced as a String. Shrinkwrap provides the WebArchive.addAsWebInfResource(File, String) method to do that.

Lines 9-10

"Static" resources need to be put at the archive's root and this can be done with WebArchive.addAsWebResource(File, String).

Line 11

Finally, the WebArchive.setWebXML(String) method can set the web deployment descriptor.

9.1.4.3 Adding library dependencies to Web archives

Shrinkwrap allows us to add Maven artifacts as libraries to web archives. These can be added with the addAsLibrary() or addAsLibraries() methods of the LibraryContainer seen above.

```
File[] files = ...
ShrinkWrap.create(WebArchive.class).addAsLibraries(files);
```

However, the greatest challenge of WAR is to get hold of those dependent libraries in the first place. As they are not available in the project itself anymore (as was the case in the "old days") but downloaded by the build system, there must be a way to plug into the latter, read required dependencies, get them and finally package them. Fortunately, Shrinkwrap provides such a way through sub-projects called resolvers: there is one for Maven and one for Gradle.

9.1.4.4 Referencing Maven dependencies

Using the Maven resolver is quite easy, as Shrinkwrap resolvers provide both BOM and POM library dependencies, which contains the API, the SPI and the Maven implementations with the relevant scopes.

Here is the associated POM excerpt:

Code 9.7 - Shrinkwrap resolvers Maven dependency configuration

```xml
<dependencyManagement>
    <dependencies>
        <dependency>
            <groupId>org.jboss.shrinkwrap.resolver</groupId>
            <artifactId>shrinkwrap-resolver-bom</artifactId>
            <version>2.1.1</version>
            <scope>import</scope>
            <type>pom</type>
        </dependency>
    </dependencies>
</dependencyManagement>
<dependencies>
    <!-- Other dependencies -->
    <dependency>
        <groupId>org.jboss.shrinkwrap.resolver</groupId>
        <artifactId>shrinkwrap-resolver-depchain</artifactId>
        <type>pom</type>
    </dependency>
</dependencies>
```

As the model of Shrinkwrap resolvers is quite complex - involving a huge class hierarchy and plenty of generics - while its usage is quite easy, let's discover it bottom-up by a simple call:

```java
Maven.resolver().resolve("org.testng:testng:6.8.8")
    .withoutTransitivity().asFile();
```

This code is pretty much self-explanatory. It resolves the Test NG JAR in version 6.8.8 as a file as per the following sequence:

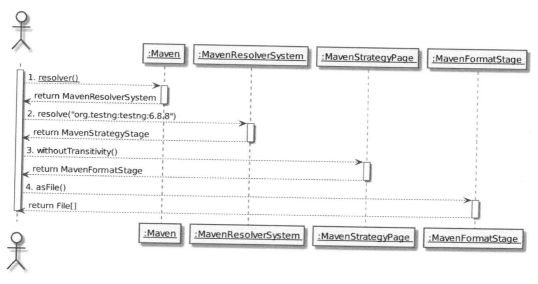

Fig. 9.6 - Simple Maven resolver sequence diagram

Here are highlights on the different phases, stage by stage:

1. Entry point

   The `org.jboss.shrinkwrap.resolver.api.maven.Maven` class and specifically its `resolver()` static method is the entry point into the Shrinkwrap resolver model. It returns a `MavenResolverSystem` instance that leads to the resolver stage.

2. Resolver stage

   The resolver stage is dedicated to the resolving of Maven artifacts (*sic*). `MavenResolverSystem` lies at the bottom of a hurge interface hierarchy providing multiple ways to achieve this. In the sample above, the method is `resolve(String)`, where the parameter is the Maven coordinates in canonical form (*groupId:artifactId:version*). It returns a `MavenStrategyStage` instance and leads to the next stage.

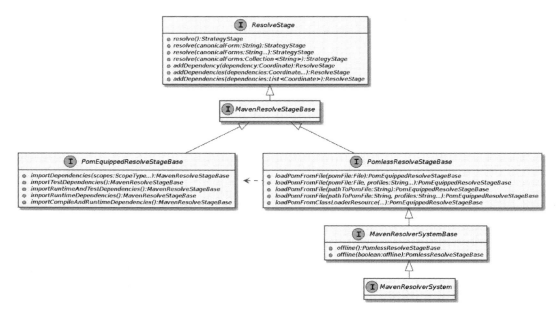

Fig. 9.7 - Maven resolve stage interface hierarchy

Beyond the sample above, there are a lot of other concerns this stage can address.

Referencing multiple artifacts

The `resolve()` method has overloaded variants to retrieve multiple artifacts at once. They accept either a `List` of strings, or even better a string varargs:

```
Maven.resolver().resolve("org.testng:testng:6.8.8",
    "org.mockito:mockito-core:1.9.5").withoutTransitivity().asFile();
```

Referencing artifacts with types and classifiers

The full form of Maven coordinates is *groupId:artifactId:packaging:version*. By default, Maven packaging is JAR so that the *packaging* part can be omitted when writing the coordinates, either in the POM or for Shrinkwrap Resolver. However, some dependencies might be of different packaging such as type pom. In order to reference such an artifact, just add the *packaging* part of the coordinates.

```
Maven.resolver()
    .resolve("org.jboss.shrinkwrap:shrinkwrap-depchain:pom:1.2.2")
    .withTransitivity().asFile();
```

Also, some artifacts are not the main result of a Maven build, but by-products. Such common artifacts include sources and JavaDoc artifacts. Referencing those kind of artifacts is achieved by appending a *classifier* coordinate, like *groupId:artifactId:packaging:classifier:version.*

```
Maven.resolver()
    .resolve("org.testng:testng:jar:sources:6.8.8")
    .withoutTransitivity().asFile();
```

Using artifact version from POM

Most, if not all the times, artifacts dependencies are already set in the POM so that setting the version in the coordinates is redundant. It might even lead to a bug as the version in the POM and in the packaged archive will be different. To let the resolver automatically handle the right version, use the `PomlessResolveStageBase.loadPomFromFile(String)` method:

```
Maven.resolver().loadPomFromFile("pom.xml")
    .resolve("org.testng:testng")
    .withoutTransitivity().asFile();
```

Other loading methods are available to let one load the POM from different locations. They may be overlooked, as the one true POM can be loaded by just calling `loadPomFromFile("pom.xml")` **provided the build is launched at the root of the project..**

Note that when one needs to reference a specific type and/or classifier while using Maven's POM dependency versions, one has to set the version coordinate part to ?.

```
Maven.resolver().loadPomFromFile("pom.xml")
    .resolve("org.jboss.shrinkwrap:shrinkwrap-depchain:pom:?")
    .withTransitivity().asFile();
```

Using profiles

Profiles are an important part of Maven's available features. Such pro-files can be activated with the help of the `loadPomFromFile(String, String...)` overrloading method. The `String...` varargs references the

profiles to be activated (or de-activated if the string starts with !) just like
the standard -P command-line option.

```
Maven.resolver().loadPomFromFile("pom.xml", "myprofile")
    .resolve("org.testng:testng")
    .withoutTransitivity().asFile();
```

Smart referencing

Once the resolver has been configured with the POM, it might sometimes be overkill to reference all required dependencies one by one.
In this case, it is good to familiarise oneself with methods from the
PomEquippedResolveStageBase interface returned by any of the over-
loading methods from PomlessResolveStageBase. The main method is
importDependencies(ScopeType) where the parameter is the Maven
scope. This way, one can import all dependencies relative to a scope (or
many scopes).

For example, calling
importDependencies(ScopeType.COMPILE, ScopeType.RUNTIME) will
only reference dependencies of scope *compile* or *runtime*. Note the return
type of the method is MavenResolveStageBase so that resolve() has to
be called just afterwards.

```
Maven.resolver().loadPomFromFile("pom.xml")
    .importDependencies(COMPILE, RUNTIME)
    .resolve().withoutTransitivity().asFile();
```

As a shortcut to define common combinations, PomEquippedResolveStageBase
also provides the importTestDependencies(), importRuntimeDependencies(),
importRuntimeAndTestDependencies() and
importCompileAndRuntimeDependencies() methods to use as shortcuts
instead of importDependencies() with scopes.

Building the complete artifact

Shrinkwrap is about building small subsets of the complete artifact
for testing purposes. However, it is sometimes necessary to build the
complete artifact. In this case, instead of duplicating all data from the
POM into API calls, Shrinkwrap provides the MavenImporter interface.
MavenImporter mimics some of the MavenResolver features.

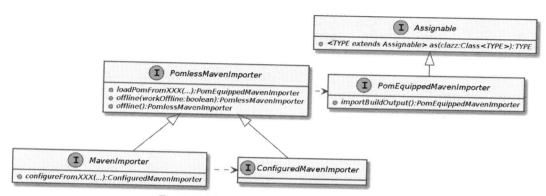

Fig. 9.8 - *Maven importer interface hierarchy*

To get hold of a `MavenImporter` instance, one should call the
`Shrinkwrap.create(Class<T>)` method, using `MavenImporter.class` as
the parameter. From this point on, creating a full-blown archive is done
with the following snippet:

```
ShrinkWrap.create(MavenImporter.class).loadPomFromFile("pom.xml")
          .importBuildOutput().as(JavaArchive.class);
```

Note that currently **only JAR and WAR artifacts can be created in
this way**, using respectively `JavaArchive.class` and `WebArchive.class`
parameters.

3. Strategy phase

This stage is responsible for determining the way we get the artifact. In the
code above, it is used to retrieve the TestNG dependency only *i.e.* with none of
the associated dependencies set in TestNG's POM. It is achieved via the help
of the `withoutTransitivity()` method and returns a `MavenFormatStage`.

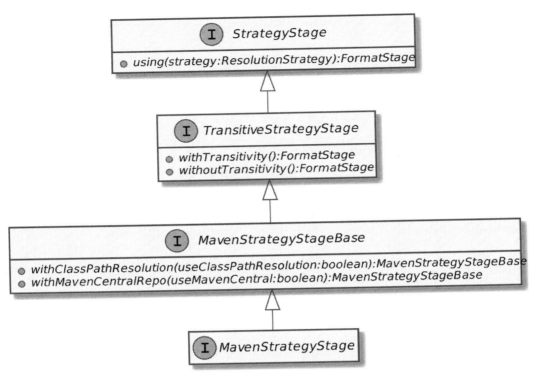

Fig. 9.9 - Maven strategy stage interface hierarchy

Two methods are available on `TransitiveStrategyStage`, `withoutTransitivity()` as seen above and `withTransitivity()`, that retrieves not only the artifact but its dependencies.

For finer-grained control, one can use the `using(ResolutionStrategy)` at the top of the hierarchy and provide the desired `ResolutionStrategy`:

- `NonTransitiveStrategy`: only artifacts explicitly referenced, this is the same as calling `withoutTransitivity()`
- `TransitiveStrategy`: both artifacts and their dependencies, the same as calling `withTransitivity()`
- `AcceptScopesStrategy`: only artifacts set in the referenced scope
- `RejectDependenciesStrategy`: prevent referenced artifacts from being retrieved
- `CombinedStrategy`: strategy implementing the Composite pattern

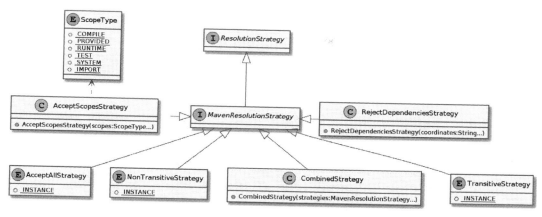

Fig. 9.10 - Resolution strategy interface hierarchy

4. Format stage

This final stage is dedicated to returning the actual dependency in the desired format.

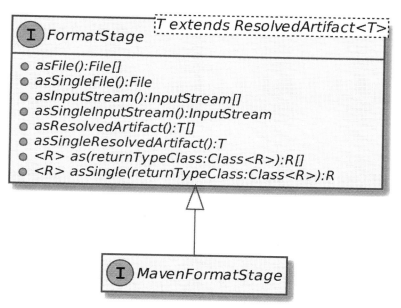

Fig. 9.11 - Format stage interface hierarchy

It is represented by the `MavenFormatStage` interface. In the previous sample call, the format was of type `File` through the `FormatStage.asFile()` method.

Other output formats are available: `InputStream`, `MavenResolvedArtifact`, `MavenCoordinate`, or any of Shrinkwrap's archive format.

There is a generic method `as(Class)` and dedicated methods for each output format.

```
Maven.resolver().loadPomFromFile("pom.xml").resolve("org.testng:testng")
    .withoutTransitivity().as(JavaArchive.class);
```

 Returning an array or a single instance There are two different flavors for each format, `asXXX()` that returns an array and `asSingleXXX()` that returns a single instance. For inclusion in Shrinkwrap archives, one can just use the returning-array flavor.

Artifact meta-data

This stage is also usable to get information about Maven dependencies through either `MavenResolvedArtifact` or `MavenCoordinate`. For this part of the model, the class diagram is the following:

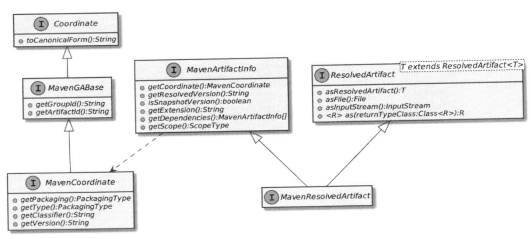

Fig. 9.12 - Maven resolved artifact interface hierarchy

9.1.4.5 Configuring a Maven Enterprise repository

Shrinkwrap resolver offers a couple of configuration features through the static
`Maven.configureResolver()` method, which returns a `ConfigurableMavenResolverSystem`
instance.

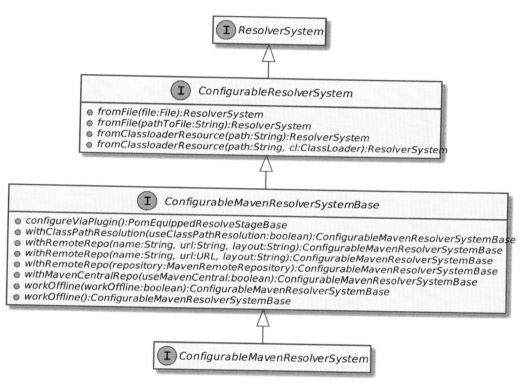

Fig. 9.13 - Configurable resolver interface hierarchy

It can be used like a regular `MavenResolverSystem` but adds more configuration
options mainly targeted at Continuous Integration. Continuous integration brings
several issues regarding usage of build systems. In particular, those systems have
to connect to the Maven Central Repository to download dependencies referenced
in the build configuration file. This repository, also known as `repo1`, is hosted *"in
the Cloud"*. There are a couple of options available to still be able to run in these
conditions.

Setting up the proxy

The first option is to configure a proxy for Continuous Integration to use. In this case, the CI server is allowed to access the Internet, but it has to go through the proxy to do so.

Maven uses proxies configured in dedicated settings files. By default, Shrinkwrap resolver will use the same settings files as Maven:

- The one located in one's home directory - `~/.m2/settings.xml`
- And the one in Maven's home directory - `$M2_HOME/conf/settings.xml`

One can configure either of these files with the proxy information. While it will be the path to walk in some organizations, other organizations will find it easier to provide a dedicated settings file inside the project and point to it.

Shrinkwrap offers two ways to point to another settings file: `fromFile()` and `fromClassLoaderResource()`. As an example, the following snippet will use the `test-settings.xml` file defined in `src/test/resources`:

```
Maven.configureResolver().fromClassloaderResource("test-settings.xml")
    .loadPomFromFile("pom.xml")
    .resolve("org.testng:testng").withoutTransitivity().asFile();
```

Setting up an Enterprise Repository

The second option is to set up a dedicated Enterprise Repository. Detailing such an infrastructure component is well beyond the scope of this book, but readers interested in this approach are welcome to check this online article: http://maven.apache.org/repository-management.html. To sum up, an Enterprise Repository acts as a proxy and a cache between the enterprise and the Internet:

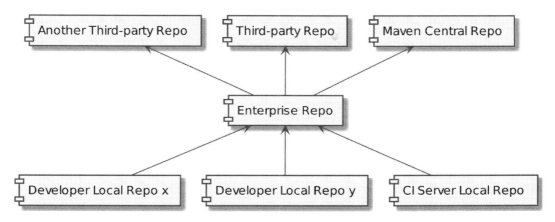

Fig. 9.14 - Enterprise Repository schema

Nowadays, nearly all providers publish their artifacts to *repo1*, but some prefer to use their own public (or private) repository, such as the SoapUI repository. Shrinkwrap is able to use any repository defined in the POM, provided the latter has been loaded as described previously.

It might happen that this repo has not been defined in the POM for a number of reasons. In this case, configuring the Enterprise Repository, or any other, can be achieved with the withRemoteRepo(String, String, String) with parameters being:

1. Repository ID *e.g.* soapui
2. Repository URL *e.g.* http://www.soapui.org/repository/maven2/
3. Repository layout, **must be** default (agreed, this is no parameter and should have been an enum)

To not access *repo1*, use the withMavenCentralRepo(boolean) method with the parameter set to false. This gives the following snippet:

```
Maven.configureResolver().withMavenCentralRepo(false)
    .withRemoteRepo("repo-id", "url://path/to/repo", "default")
    .resolve("org.testng:testng").withoutTransitivity().asFile();
```

Use the local repository only

To prevent online access (similar to Maven's -o command-line parameter), use the workOffline() method. This will force Shrinkwrap to rely on the machine's local repository only. A way must be found to set all required dependencies in the local repo in the first place or Maven dependency resolution will fail.

This section concludes the description of the Shrinkwrap API, which allows to create fully-configurable archives.

9.2 Arquillian

As it is able to create the artifact corresponding to the SUT, Shrinkrap plays a huge role in Integration Testing Java EE applications. But just as artifact creation is only a part of Integration Testing, Shrinkwrap is only a part of a greater whole. Its umbrella project is called Arquillian and allows for things such as downloading application servers, managing their lifecycle, deploying the created artifact on them and finally testing the whole.

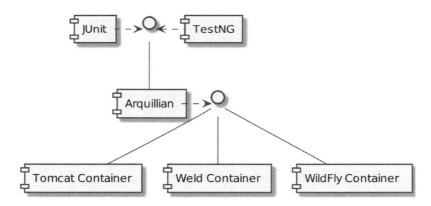

Fig. 9.15 - Arquillian architecture overview

Arquillian is fully modularized, which makes it integrated with JUnit and TestNG, and also provides out-of-the-box adaptors to the most widespread application servers. The exact choice of the testing framework and application servers to deploy on can be configured through the Maven POM and a dedicated `arquillian.xml` configuration file.

9.2.1 Preparing for Arquillian usage

As with Spring and Shrinkwrap, Arquillian provides a BOM to manage all dependency versions to be compatible:

```
<dependency>
    <groupId>org.jboss.arquillian</groupId>
    <artifactId>arquillian-bom</artifactId>
    <version>1.1.5.Final</version>
    <type>pom</type>
    <scope>import</scope>
</dependency>
```

To add the TestNG adapter dependency, add the following dependency:

```
<dependency>
    <groupId>org.jboss.arquillian.testng</groupId>
    <artifactId>arquillian-testng-container</artifactId>
    <scope>test</scope>
</dependency>
```

Adding those snippets to the POM enables creating the test class.

9.2.2 Creating the test class

Creating the test class only requires a few steps:

1. Extend the `org.jboss.arquillian.testng.Arquillian` class to benefit from out-of-the-box Arquillian/TestNG integration. Alternatively, annotate the class with `@RunWith(org.jboss.arquillian.junit.Arquillian)` to use JUnit instead.

2. Create a static method that creates the desired Java EE archive (JAR, WAR, EAR, etc.) with the Shrinkwrap API, as seen in the above section.

3. Annotate it with org.jboss.arquillian.api.Deployment to let Arquillian deploy the archive just prior to test execution.

4. Add any required instance as class attributes and annotate them with the standard @javax.inject.Inject annotation.

This is the corresponding template:

```
1   public class MyArquillianTest extends Arquillian {
2
3       @Inject
4       private MyService myService;
5
6       @Deployment
7       public static JavaArchive createJar() {
8           return ShrinkWrap.create(JavaArchive.class);
9           // Probably add resources to archive there
10      }
11
12      @Test
13      public void should_do_this() {
14          myService.doThis();
15          Assert.assertThat(...);
16      }
17  }
```

9.2.3 Testing in-container

This chapter aims to show how to test code in-container, but so far containers have been left out of the picture. The goal of this section is to configure deployed-to containers and the way to deploy into one such (or multiple) container(s).

What is a container anyway?

Java EE defines several containers: web containers, Enterprise JavaBean *i.e.* EJB containers and more recently Context and Dependency Injection *i.e.* CDI containers. A container is an environment that knows how to respectively run Servlets, EJBs and CDI beans.

9.2.3.1 Container adapter types

Containers come in 3 different kinds:

Embedded

An embedded container is automatically downloaded by Arquillian prior to the test, and it is run inside the same Java Virtual Machine along with the test. The main advantage of using an embedded container is that it decouples tests from any container dependency; its main disadvantage is that the initial download time might be very big - depending on the nature of the container.

Remote

A remote container is completely independent from the test, it exists before test execution and will stay after it. "Remote" might be a slightly misleading term, as nothing prevents the Java EE container and the test-running container to be hosted on the same machine. In all cases, remote requires a communication channel between both containers, such as HTTP. Arquillian takes care of the communication process.

Managed

A managed container is a kind of remote container that can (must) be started and stopped explictly during test execution. Lifecycle management can be configured, while Arquillian handles the nitty-gritty underlying communication.

Arquillian manages containers through abstractions known as container adapters. Available container adapters are the following:

Table 9.1 - Available container adapters

Container	Version	Embedded	Remote	Managed	Maven coordinates pattern
Weld SE	1.0	☒			weld-se
	1.1	☒			
Weld EE	1.1	☒			weld-ee
Apache OpenWebBeans	1.0	☒		☒	openwebbeans
Apache OpenEJB	3.1	☒			openejb
Apache Tomcat	5.5			☒	tomcat
	6.0	☒	☒	☒	
	7.0	☒	☒	☒	
Apache TomEE ‡	1.0.0	☒	☒		tomee
	1.5.2	☒	☒		
	1.6.0.2	☒	☒		
	1.7.1	☒	☒		
Jetty	6.1	☒			jetty
	7.0	☒			
JBoss AS	4.2		☒	☒	jbossas
	5		☒		
	5.1		☒	☒	
	6.0	☒	☒	☒	
	7.0		☒	☒	
	7.1 †		☒	☒	
	7.2 †			☒	
WildFly	8.1 †	☒			
Oracle GlassFish	3.1	☒	☒	☒	glassfish
Oracle WebLogic Server	10.3		☒		wls
	12.1		☒		
IBM WebSphere	7		☒		was
	8	☒	☒		

†: provided by JBoss ‡: provided by Apache TomEE

Arquillian provided adapters

Adapters that are not explicitly marked as provided by third-parties are provided by the Arquillian project. Maven coordinates of those adapters require the following dependency:

```
<dependency>
    <groupId>org.jboss.arquillian.container</groupId>
    <artifactId>...</artifactId>
    <scope>${adapter.version}</scope>
</dependency>
```

The artifact ID adopts the `arquillian-${artifact-pattern}-${adapter-type}-${container-version}` pattern with:

- `${artifact-pattern}` is the reference pattern found in the above table
- `${adapter-type}` depends on the specific container adapter, `embedded`, `remote` or `managed`,
- `${container-version}` is the container's major.minor version. The catch is that if minor version is `0`, then this is "rounded down" to the major version *e.g.* version 7.0 will be translated as 7

Here are some examples:

- Weld SE 1.1 artifact ID - which is only available as embedded, is `arquillian-weld-se-embedded-1.1`
- To reference a remote Tomcat 7, use `arquillian-tomcat-remote-7`

JBoss provided adapters

For artifacts provided by JBoss (marked as † in the table above), the Maven dependency template looks like:

```
<dependency>
    <groupId>org.jboss.as</groupId>
    <artifactId>...</artifactId>
    <version>${jboss-as.version}</version>
</dependency>
```

The artifact ID in turn adopts the
`${artifact-pattern}-${adapter-type}-arquillian-container` pattern, while
`${jboss-as.version}` is the version of the JBoss Application Server suffixed
by `.Final`. For example, for the JBoss AS 7.1.0 managed adapter, the dependency is the following:

```
<dependency>
    <groupId>org.jboss.as</groupId>
    <artifactId>jboss-as-arquillian-container-managed</artifactId>
    <version>7.1.0.Final</version>
</dependency>
```

TomEE provided adapters

For TomEE artifacts, the template is:

```
<dependency>
    <groupId>org.apache.openejb</groupId>
    <artifactId>...</artifactId>
    <version>${tomee.version}</version>
</dependency>
```

The artifact ID is `arquillian-tomee-${adapter-type}` and `${tomee.version}`
directly references the TomEE container version. Thus, the Maven dependency
for the TomEE embedded adapter is:

```
<dependency>
    <groupId>org.apache.openejb</groupId>
    <artifactId>arquillian-tomee-embedded</artifactId>
    <version>1.7.1</version>
</dependency>
```

9.2.3.2 Simplest Arquillian test

At this point, it is possible to finally run our first Arquillian test. As an illustration, let's create a basic CDI injection configuration with the Weld engine (Weld is CDI's reference implementation). The source code is the following:

Code 9.8 - Basic CDI example code

```
1   public class InjectedObject {}
2
3   public class InjectableService {
4
5       @javax.inject.Inject
6       private InjectedObject injectedObject;
7
8       public InjectedObject getInjectedObject() {
9           return injectedObject;
10      }
11  }
```

This configuration is very straightforward: the `InjectableService` gets an injected `InjectedObject` instance. The corresponding POM is this one:

Code 9.9 - Basic POM

```
1   <?xml version="1.0" encoding="UTF-8"?>
2   <project ...>
3       <modelVersion>4.0.0</modelVersion>
4       <groupId>ch.frankel.integrationtest.javaee</groupId>
5       <artifactId>simplearquillian</artifactId>
6       <version>1.0.0</version>
7       <build>
8           <plugins>
9               <plugin>
10                  <artifactId>maven-failsafe-plugin</artifactId>
11                  <version>2.18</version>
12                  <executions>
13                      <execution>
```

```
14                               <id>integrationtest</id>
15                               <goals>
16                                   <goal>integration-test</goal>
17                               </goals>
18                               <phase>integration-test</phase>
19                           </execution>
20                       </executions>
21                   </plugin>
22               </plugins>
23           </build>
24           <dependencyManagement>
25               <dependencies>
26                   <dependency>
27                       <groupId>org.jboss.arquillian</groupId>
28                       <artifactId>arquillian-bom</artifactId>
29                       <version>1.1.5.Final</version>
30                       <type>pom</type>
31                       <scope>import</scope>
32                   </dependency>
33               </dependencies>
34           </dependencyManagement>
35           <dependencies>
36               <dependency>
37                   <groupId>org.jboss.weld</groupId>
38                   <artifactId>weld-core</artifactId>
39                   <version>2.2.5.Final</version>
40               </dependency>
41               <dependency>
42                   <groupId>org.jboss.arquillian.testng</groupId>
43                   <artifactId>arquillian-testng-container</artifactId>
44                   <scope>test</scope>
45               </dependency>
46               <dependency>
47                   <groupId>org.testng</groupId>
48                   <artifactId>testng</artifactId>
49                   <version>6.8.8</version>
50                   <scope>test</scope>
51               </dependency>
```

```
52          <dependency>
53              <groupId>org.jboss.arquillian.container</groupId>
54              <artifactId>arquillian-weld-se-embedded-1.1</artifactId>
55              <version>1.0.0.CR8</version>
56              <scope>test</scope>
57          </dependency>
58      </dependencies>
59  </project>
```

Line 9-21

As seen in *Chapter 4 - Automated testing*, the Maven Failsafe plugin has to be configured to run integration tests in the correct Maven phase.

Line 26-32

The Arquillian BOM is necessary to set the correct dependency versions instead of just setting the version on `arquillian-testng-container`. Don't forget to set the type to `pom` and the scope to `import`.

Lines 36-40

The simplest CDI engine is Weld. The `weld-core` dependency transitively adds the required `javax.inject` JAR on the classpath and makes the `@Inject` annotation available.

Lines 41-51

TestNG and Arquillian's TestNG API, the first is required to use test framework, the second to hook into Arquillian with it.

Lines 52-57

Weld's Arquillian container, since Weld is the CDI implementation to use. Should other CDI implementations be necessary, they should be written along this one.

The test will simply check the expected injection takes place.

Code 9.10 - Simple CDI smoke test

```java
1    import org.jboss.arquillian.container.test.api.Deployment;
2    import org.jboss.arquillian.testng.Arquillian;
3    import org.jboss.shrinkwrap.api.spec.JavaArchive;
4    import org.testng.annotations.Test;
5
6    import javax.inject.Inject;
7
8    import static org.jboss.shrinkwrap.api.ShrinkWrap.create;
9    import static org.jboss.shrinkwrap.api.asset.EmptyAsset.INSTANCE;
10   import static org.testng.Assert.assertNotNull;
11
12   public class InjectableServiceIT extends Arquillian {
13
14       @Inject
15       private InjectableService injectableService;
16
17       @Deployment
18       public static JavaArchive createJar() {
19           return create(JavaArchive.class).
20                   addPackage(InjectableService.class.getPackage()).
21                   addAsManifestResource(INSTANCE, "beans.xml");
22       }
23
24       @Test
25       public void shoud_be_injected() {
26           assertNotNull(injectableService.getInjectedObject());
27       }
28   }
```

Line 12

In order for the magic to happen, the test class has to extend the provided Arquillian class for TestNG. JUnit users have a specific Arquillian runner in their dedicated dependency.

Line 14-15

Any bean available to the CDI engine can be injected. In this case, let's aim for the `InjectableService` instance to be able to test it.

Line 17-22

As seen in the previous Shrinkwrap section, this method creates the archive for Arquillian to deploy. Hints are the `@Deployment` annotation, along with the `static` modifier, and probably the IDE warning that this method is used nowhere in the codebase. The archive is a simple JAR, with every class belonging to the same package as `InjectableService`, so `InjectedObject` is packaged along as well. Finally, note CDI **must** be activated by packaging a simple empty `beans.xml` file in the `META-INF` folder: this is the goal of line 21.

Line 24-27

The meat of the test, as the code above was only to set everything up. Note that if injection does not happen, existing CDI implementations will throw an exception and fail to start the container. However, a test has to assert something and this one can be considered a smoke test, a way to check injection works before going further.

Switching from one container adapter to another is quite easy, as the promise of Arquillian is to keep standard code and tests and just change the container adapter - the dependencies. As a simple example, let's try TomEE Embedded instead of Weld.

Code 9.11 - Using Tomcat Embedded container adapter

```
1   <dependency>
2       <groupId>org.apache.openejb</groupId>
3       <artifactId>arquillian-tomee-embedded</artifactId>
4       <version>1.7.1</version>
5       <exclusions>
6           <exclusion>
7               <groupId>org.jboss.arquillian.junit</groupId>
8               <artifactId>arquillian-junit-container</artifactId>
9           </exclusion>
10      </exclusions>
11  </dependency>
12  <dependency>
13      <groupId>org.jboss.arquillian.testng</groupId>
```

```
14          <artifactId>arquillian-testng-container</artifactId>
15          <scope>test</scope>
16      </dependency>
17      <dependency>
18          <groupId>org.testng</groupId>
19          <artifactId>testng</artifactId>
20          <version>6.8.8</version>
21          <scope>test</scope>
22      </dependency>
23      <dependency>
24          <groupId>org.apache.openejb</groupId>
25          <artifactId>tomee-embedded</artifactId>
26          <version>1.7.1</version>
27          <scope>test</scope>
28      </dependency>
29  </dependencies>
30  </project>
```

Just replacing the dependencies in the POM is enough, Arquillian will launch the test within the TomEE container instead of Weld. The only twist is to exclude `arquillian-junit-container` from `arquillian-tomee-embedded` as the latter has a direct dependency on the former (and TestNG is used). This is not necessary if one uses JUnit, though.

9.2.3.3 Configuring adapters

The previous test is quite straightforward. In particular, neither the Weld container nor the Embedded Tomcat adapters require any configuration: the test just runs as it is.

However, some specific adapters do need some configuration, *e.g.* the HTTP port number or the container install directory for managed containers. Of course, those configuration parameters are dependent on each specific adapter. All have to be set in a dedicated `arqullian.xml` file located at the root of `src/test/resources`. The corresponding XML Schema is `http://www.jboss.org/schema/arquillian/arquillian_1_0.xsd`, its overview is the following:

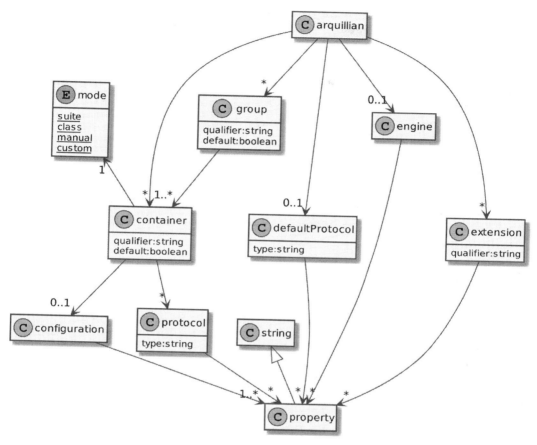

Fig. 9.16 - Arquillian XML model overview

Code 9.12 - arquillian.xml sample for Tomcat Embedded

```
1   <container qualifier="tomee" default="true">
2       <configuration>
3           <property name="httpPort">-1</property>
4           <property name="stopPort">-1</property>
5       </configuration>
6   </container>
```

The most important element is `container`, and its main (required) attribute is `qualifier` - a short descriptive label to reference it.

9.2.3.4 Testing on multiple containers

The most interesting part of Arquillian is to run tests on multiple containers to ensure 100% compatibility on those. This is easily achieved with Maven profiles (http://maven.apache.org/guides/introduction/introduction-to-profiles.html): profiles are portions of the POM that can be activated based on a flag - the profile name, set on the command-line. The following will activate the `myprofile` profile (if it exists):

```
mvn integration-test -Pmyprofile
```

Testing on different containers just requires putting all dependencies of each adapter into a dedicated profile in the POM. Given the previous two Weld and TomEE embedded adapters, this translates into the following POM:

Code 9.13 - Multiple container adapters POM

```
1  <?xml version="1.0" encoding="UTF-8"?>
2  <project ...>
3      ...
4      <dependencyManagement>
5          <dependencies>
6              <dependency>
7                  <groupId>org.jboss.arquillian</groupId>
8                  <artifactId>arquillian-bom</artifactId>
9                  <version>1.1.5.Final</version>
10                 <type>pom</type>
11                 <scope>import</scope>
12             </dependency>
13         </dependencies>
14     </dependencyManagement>
15     <dependencies>
16         <dependency>
17             <groupId>org.jboss.arquillian.testng</groupId>
18             <artifactId>arquillian-testng-container</artifactId>
19             <scope>test</scope>
20         </dependency>
21         <dependency>
```

```
22          <groupId>org.testng</groupId>
23          <artifactId>testng</artifactId>
24          <version>6.8.8</version>
25          <scope>test</scope>
26      </dependency>
27  </dependencies>
28  <profiles>
29      <profile>
30          <id>weld</id>
31          <dependencies>
32              <dependency>
33                  <groupId>org.jboss.weld</groupId>
34                  <artifactId>weld-core</artifactId>
35                  <version>2.2.5.Final</version>
36              </dependency>
37              <dependency>
38                  <groupId>org.jboss.arquillian.container</groupId>
39                  <artifactId>arquillian-weld-se-embedded-1.1</artifactId>
40                  <version>1.0.0.CR8</version>
41                  <scope>test</scope>
42              </dependency>
43          </dependencies>
44      </profile>
45      <profile>
46          <id>tomee</id>
47          <dependencies>
48              <dependency>
49                  <groupId>org.apache.openejb</groupId>
50                  <artifactId>arquillian-tomee-embedded</artifactId>
51                  <version>1.7.1</version>
52                  <exclusions>
53                      <exclusion>
54                       <groupId>org.jboss.arquillian.junit</groupId>
55                       <artifactId>arquillian-junit-container</artifactId>
56                      </exclusion>
57                  </exclusions>
58              </dependency>
59              <dependency>
```

```
60              <groupId>org.apache.openejb</groupId>
61              <artifactId>tomee-embedded</artifactId>
62              <version>1.7.1</version>
63              <scope>test</scope>
64          </dependency>
65        </dependencies>
66      </profile>
67    </profiles>
68 </project>
```

Lines 29-44 set up a weld profile, while lines 45-66 set up a tomee one and each profile declare dependencies relevant only for their own container adapter. Note lines 15-27 declare dependencies common to both adapters.

Launching tests for each container adapter is done with the following command-lines:

```
mvn integration-test -Pweld
mvn integration-test -Ptomee
```

9.2.4 Other Arquillian use-cases

So far, Arquillian has been used to test CDI usage, but the Java EE platfom is far richer than just only CDI.

9.2.4.1 Enterprise Java Beans

Enterprise Java Beans (also known as EJBs) are a major part of Java EE since the platform's inception. EJBs are available in different flavors: *Session*, *Entity* and *Message-driven*. With CDI, each new release of the EJB specifications blurs the line between Session EJBs and CDI beans. At the time of the writing of this book, they still both are different beasts but similar enough to use nearly the same test code. Here is a port of the above code using the EJB specification instead of CDI:

Code 9.14 - Basic EJB example code

```
1   @javax.ejb.Stateless
2   public class InjectedEjb {}
3
4   @javax.ejb.Stateless
5   public class InjectableEjb {
6
7       @javax.ejb.EJB
8       private InjectedEjb injectedEjb;
9
10      public InjectedEjb getInjectedEjb() {
11          return injectedEjb;
12      }
13  }
```

There are two slight differences: while CDI beans are automatically registered when the bean is on the classpath, EJBs have to be annotated with @Stateless (or @Stateful) to be scanned. On the caller class side, @Inject is simply replaced with @EJB. The test itself is quite similar to the previous CDI test:

Code 9.15 - Simple EJB smoke test

```
1   import org.jboss.arquillian.container.test.api.Deployment;
2   import org.jboss.arquillian.testng.Arquillian;
3   import org.jboss.shrinkwrap.api.spec.JavaArchive;
4   import org.testng.annotations.Test;
5
6   import javax.ejb.EJB;
7
8   import static org.jboss.shrinkwrap.api.ShrinkWrap.create;
9   import static org.testng.Assert.assertNotNull;
10
11  public class InjectableEjbIT extends Arquillian {
12
13      @EJB
14      private InjectableEjb injectableEjb;
```

```
15
16      @Deployment
17      public static JavaArchive createJar() {
18          return create(JavaArchive.class).
19                  addPackage(InjectableEjb.class.getPackage());
20      }
21
22      @Test
23      public void shoud_be_injected() {
24          assertNotNull(injectableEjb.getInjectedEjb());
25      }
26  }
```

9.2.4.2 JAX-WS

Web Services play an important role in today's distributed systems. It lets applications talk to one another in an agnostic way. SOAP is a protocol for Web Services using XML and Java EE enables SOAP Web Services in a elegant way through the Java API for XML-Based Web Services (https://jax-ws.java.net/) also known as JAX-WS. For a tutorial on JAX-WS, please refer to the Oracle documentation: http://docs.oracle.com/javaee/6/tutorial/doc/bnayn.html.

Here is some basic JAX-WS code that returns "ping" when it is called:

Code 9.16 - Basic JAX-WS example code

```
1   @javax.jws.WebService
2   public interface Ping {
3
4       String NAMESPACE = "http://integrationtesting.net/";
5       String SERVICE = "PingService";
6       String PORT = "PingPort";
7
8       String ping();
9   }
10
11  @javax.jws.WebService(
12      portName = Ping.PORT,
```

```
13        serviceName = Ping.SERVICE,
14        targetNamespace = Ping.NAMESPACE,
15        endpointInterface = "Ping"
16    )
17    public class PingWebService implements Ping {
18
19        public String ping() {
20            return "ping";
21        }
22    }
```

Lines 1-2

The Ping super-interface is defined and annotated with @javax.jws.WebService.

Lines 4-6

Constants are defined. Though not necessary, creating those constants instead of using strings directly allows their values to be used in both the implementation and the test with no chance of typos.

Lines 11-16

The implementation also has to be annotated with @WebService. The only really required attribute is endpointInterface, which should be set to the fully qualified name of the Ping interface defined on line 2. Other annotation attributes are used to create the Web Service Definition Language file. They are not that necessary, but default values are well... default - here they are:

- targetNamespace is set to the concatenation of http:// and the package name
- serviceName is set to the concatenation of the class name and Service
- portName is set to the concatenation of the class name and Port

Line 17-21

PingWebService implements the Ping interface defined previously on line 2.

A good thing about the Oracle JDK is that it provides an embedded JAX-WS engine that can be used to test the previous code. Here is a very summarized model:

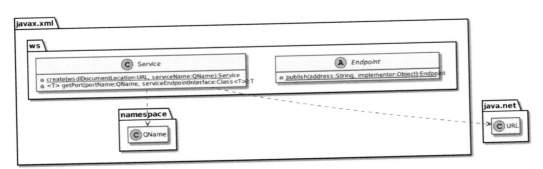

Fig. 9.17 - JDK embedded JAX-WS model

Given this model, the following code tests the JAX-WS code:

Code 9.17 - Simple JAX-WS integration test

```
1    import org.jboss.arquillian.testng.Arquillian;
2    import org.testng.annotations.*;
3
4    import javax.xml.namespace.QName;
5    import javax.xml.ws.*;
6    import java.net.*;
7
8    import static org.testng.Assert.assertEquals;
9
10   public class PingWebServiceIT {
11
12       private static final String SERVICE_URL = "http://localhost:8080/ping";
13       private static final String WSDL_URL = SERVICE_URL + "?wsdl";
14       private Endpoint endpoint;
15
16       @BeforeMethod
17       protected void setUp() {
18           endpoint = Endpoint.publish(SERVICE_URL, new PingWebService());
19       }
20
21       @Test
22       public void should_ping() throws MalformedURLException {
23           URL wsdl = new URL(WSDL_URL);
```

```
24      QName serviceQn = new QName(Ping.NAMESPACE, Ping.SERVICE);
25      QName portQn = new QName(Ping.NAMESPACE, Ping.PORT);
26      Service service = Service.create(wsdl, serviceQn);
27      Ping port = service.getPort(portQn, Ping.class);
28      assertEquals(port.ping(), "ping");
29    }
30
31    @AfterMethod
32    protected  void tearDown() {
33        endpoint.stop();
34    }
35 }
```

The previous test is an integration test, but is not run inside the container. Thus, it cannot really guarantee the code will run as intended in-container. To achieve that, Arquillian is needed. First, the problem of the JAX-WS implementation should be answered. For example, neither Tomcat nor TomEE provide such an implementation out-of-the-box.

 TomEE+ provides Apache CXF as JAX-WS implementation but is unfortunately not available as a Maven dependency.

For simplicity's sake, let's use the JAX-WS Reference Implementation - Metro (https://jax-ws.java.net/). It is available as a Maven dependency with coordinates com.sun.xml.ws:jaxws-rt. As TomEE is no use, it is better to use a simple Tomcat. As an example, for the combination of the Tomcat container and the Metro library, the POM dependencies are the following (respectively lines 1-18 for the former and lines 19-24 for the latter):

Metro requires a specific sun-jaxws.xml configuration file, to map URLs to implementation classes, so that Metro knows to which class to direct incoming requests. For the previous PingWebService, there is only one. Here is the corresponding configuration file:

Code 9.18 - Tomcat and Metro Maven dependencies

```
1   <dependency>
2       <groupId>org.apache.tomcat.embed</groupId>
3       <artifactId>tomcat-embed-core</artifactId>
4       <version>7.0.56</version>
5       <scope>test</scope>
6   </dependency>
7   <dependency>
8       <groupId>org.apache.tomcat.embed</groupId>
9       <artifactId>tomcat-embed-jasper</artifactId>
10      <version>7.0.56</version>
11      <scope>test</scope>
12  </dependency>
13  <dependency>
14      <groupId>org.apache.tomcat.embed</groupId>
15      <artifactId>tomcat-embed-logging-juli</artifactId>
16      <version>7.0.56</version>
17      <scope>test</scope>
18  </dependency>
19  <dependency>
20      <groupId>com.sun.xml.ws</groupId>
21      <artifactId>jaxws-rt</artifactId>
22      <version>2.2.8</version>
23      <scope>test</scope>
24  </dependency>
```

Code 9.19 - Metro configuration file sample

```
1   <?xml version="1.0" encoding="UTF-8"?>
2   <endpoints xmlns="http://java.sun.com/xml/ns/jax-ws/ri/runtime"
3             version="2.0">
4       <endpoint name="Ping" implementation="PingWebService"
5                 url-pattern="/PingService"/>
6   </endpoints>
```

Likewise, Metro offers a dedicated servlet, as well as a context listener, that are to be configured in the web deployment descriptor. For testing purpose, it can either be the final web.xml or a test one dedicated to Metro, or one even one solely dedicated to the Ping web service. For better confidence in the code, it is advised to choose the first option, for faster tests, the latter. The following is a web deployment descriptor specific to Ping:

Code 9.20 - Metro web deployment descriptor

```
1   <web-app ...>
2       <servlet>
3           <servlet-name>MetroWS</servlet-name>
4           <servlet-class>
5               com.sun.xml.ws.transport.http.servlet.WSServlet
6           </servlet-class>
7       </servlet>
8       <servlet-mapping>
9           <servlet-name>MetroWS</servlet-name>
10          <url-pattern>/</url-pattern>
11      </servlet-mapping>
12      <listener>
13          <listener-class>
14              com.sun.xml.ws.transport.http.servlet.WSServletContextListener
15          </listener-class>
16      </listener>
17  </web-app>
```

The overall project structure is this:

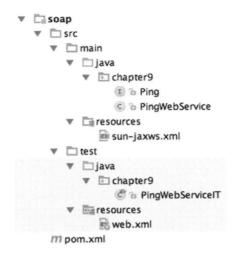

Fig. 9.18 - JAX-WS project structure

Before going further, there is one problem to solve. The entry-point of the test should not be the test method itself as for previous Arquillian tests but the corresponding URL, as JAX-WS is based on them. In order to get hold of the reference, one has to tell Arquillian to inject it. This is achieved by annotating a URL parameter of the test method with @ArquillianResource:

```
@Test
public void test_method(@ArquillianResource URL url)
```

URL injection and TestNG

Using the previous snippet with TestNG will produce this error message:

```
org.testng.TestNGException:
Method test_method requires 1 parameters
but 0 were supplied in the @Test annotation.
```

JUnit Arquillian's runner is able to inject the URL but TestNG requires the provided `Arquillian.ARQUILLIAN_DATA_PROVIDER` data provider on the @Test annotation for injection to take place.

```
@Test(dataProvider = ARQUILLIAN_DATA_PROVIDER)
public void test_method(@ArquillianResource URL url)
```

Given the same production code, the new test becomes:

Code 9.21 - JAX-WS Arquillian in-container test

```
1   import org.jboss.arquillian.container.test.api.Deployment;
2   import org.jboss.arquillian.test.api.ArquillianResource;
3   import org.jboss.arquillian.testng.Arquillian;
4   import org.jboss.shrinkwrap.api.spec.WebArchive;
5   import org.testng.annotations.Test;
6
7   import javax.xml.namespace.QName;
8   import javax.xml.ws.Service;
9   import java.net.*;
10
11  import static org.jboss.shrinkwrap.api.ShrinkWrap.create;
12  import static org.testng.Assert.assertEquals;
13
14  public class PingWebServiceIT extends Arquillian {
15
16      public static final String WSDL = "?wsdl";
17
18      @Deployment(testable = false)
```

```
19    public static WebArchive createWar() {
20        return create(WebArchive.class).addPackage(Ping.class.getPackage())
21            .addAsWebInfResource("sun-jaxws.xml").setWebXML("ping-web.xml");
22    }
23
24    @Test(dataProvider = ARQUILLIAN_DATA_PROVIDER)
25    public void should_ping(@ArquillianResource URL deploymentUrl)
26            throws MalformedURLException {
27        URL wsdl = new URL(deploymentUrl, Ping.SERVICE + WSDL);
28        QName serviceQn = new QName(Ping.NAMESPACE, Ping.SERVICE);
29        QName portQn = new QName(Ping.NAMESPACE, Ping.PORT);
30        Service service = Service.create(wsdl, serviceQn);
31        Ping port = service.getPort(portQn, Ping.class);
32        assertEquals(port.ping(), "ping");
33    }
34 }
```

Line 14

As for all previous Arquillian tests, the test class has to extend `Arquillian`

Line 18

There is a bug with the Arquillian TestNG code that require `testable = false`: https://issues.jboss.org/browse/ARQ-1376

Lines 19-22

The usual Shrinkwrap archive creation method, which assembles necessary classes - the production code and test code, and resources - the Metro configuration file and the webapp deployment descriptor.

Lines 24-33

The testing code proper. It is very similar to the not-in-container testing code 9.17 above, the difference being the URL does not come from a constant but injected by the container itself.

9.3 Summary

The chapter described how to test Java EE code in-container. This is achieved by using two different libraries:

- Shrinkwrap allows to create Java EE archives such as JAR, WAR, etc. with a fluent API
- Arquillian is the test framework proper. This enables injection of Java EE resources in the test class: CDI beans, EJB, URL, etc. Besides injection, the Arquillian project also provides integration modules for both JUnit and TestNG. Finally, Arquillian has plenty of adapters for every widespread application container such as Tomcat, TomEE, JBoss and the like.

Appendix A: Tools

Root frameworks

JUnit

"JUnit is a simple framework to write repeatable tests. It is an instance of the xUnit architecture for unit testing frameworks."

- GitHub
- Wiki
- Download
- v4.10 JavaDoc
- Maven artifact

```
<dependency>
    <groupId>junit</groupId>
    <artifactId>junit</artifactId>
    <version>4.11</version>
    <scope>test</scope>
</dependency>
```

TestNG

"TestNG is a testing framework inspired from JUnit and NUnit but introducing some new functionalities that make it more powerful and easier to use."

- GitHub

- Documentation
- Download
- JavaDoc
- Maven artifact

```
<dependency>
    <groupId>org.testng</groupId>
    <artifactId>testng</artifactId>
    <version>6.8.7</version>
    <scope>test</scope>
</dependency>
```

Assertion frameworks

FEST-Assert

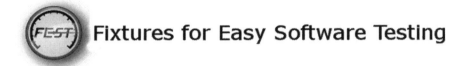 Fixtures for Easy Software Testing

"FEST-Assert provides a fluent interface for assertions."

- GitHub
- Download
- Documentation
- Maven artifact

```
<dependency>
    <groupId>org.easytesting</groupId>
    <artifactId>fest-assert-core</artifactId>
    <version>2.0M8</version>
    <scope>test</scope>
</dependency>
```

Hamcrest

"Hamcrest is a library of matchers, which can be combined in to create flexible expressions of intent in tests."

- GitHub
- Download
- JavaDoc
- Maven artifact

```
<dependency>
    <groupId>org.hamcrest</groupId>
    <artifactId>hamcrest-all</artifactId>
    <version>1.3</version>
    <scope>test</scope>
</dependency>
```

AssertJ

"AssertJ core is a Java library that provides a fluent interface for writing assertions. Its main goal is to improve test code readability and make maintenance of tests easier. AssertJ core provides assertions for JDK standard types, it requires Java SE 6.0 or later and can be used with either JUnit or TestNG."

- GitHub
- Documentation
- JavaDoc
- Maven artifact

```
<dependency>
    <groupId>org.assertj</groupId>
    <artifactId>assertj-core</artifactId>
    <version>1.6.0</version>
    <scope>test</scope>
</dependency>
```

Mocking frameworks

Mockito

"Mockito is a mocking framework that tastes really good. It lets you write beautiful tests with clean & simple API. Mockito doesn't give you hangover because the tests are very readable and they produce clean verification errors."

- GitHub
- Documentation
- JavaDoc
- Maven artifact

```xml
<dependency>
    <groupId>org.mockito</groupId>
    <artifactId>mockito-core</artifactId>
    <version>1.9.5</version>
    <scope>test</scope>
</dependency>
```

PowerMock

"PowerMock is a framework that extend other mock libraries [...] with more powerful capabilities. PowerMock uses a custom classloader and bytecode manipulation to enable mocking of static methods, constructors, final classes and methods, private methods, removal of static initializers and more."

- Google Code
- Documentation

- Download
- JavaDoc
- Maven artifact

```xml
<dependency>
    <groupId>org.powermock</groupId>
    <artifactId>powermock-module-testng</artifactId>
    <version>1.5.2</version>
    <scope>test</scope>
</dependency>
<dependency>
    <groupId>org.powermock</groupId>
    <artifactId>powermock-api-mockito</artifactId>
    <version>1.5.2</version>
    <scope>test</scope>
</dependency>
```

Fake API frameworks

MockRunner

"Mockrunner is a lightweight framework for unit testing applications in the J2EE environment. It supports servlets, filters, tag classes and Struts actions and forms. Furthermore it includes a JDBC, a JMS and a JCA test framework and can be used in conjunction with MockEJB to test EJB based applications."

- GitHub
- Documentation
- Download
- JMS JavaDoc
- JMS Maven artifact

```
<dependency>
    <groupId>com.mockrunner</groupId>
    <artifactId>mockrunner-jms</artifactId>
    <version>0.4.6</version>
    <scope>test</scope>
</dependency>
```

Fake Resource frameworks

DBUnit

"DbUnit is a JUnit extension (also usable with Ant) targeted at database-driven projects that, among other things, puts your database into a known state between test runs. This is an excellent way to avoid the myriad of problems that can occur when one test case corrupts the database and causes subsequent tests to fail or exacerbate the damage.

DbUnit has the ability to export and import your database data to and from XML datasets. Since version 2.0, DbUnit can also work with very large datasets when used in streaming mode. DbUnit can also help you to verify that your database data match an expected set of values."

- Sourceforge
- Documentation
- Download
- JavaDoc
- Maven artifact

```
<dependency>
    <groupId>org.dbunit</groupId>
    <artifactId>dbunit</artifactId>
    <version>2.4.9</version>
    <scope>test</scope>
</dependency>
```

DBSetup

> *"DbSetup is a free, open-source Java API that helps you setup your database data to execute DAO/Repository unit tests. It plays in the same league as tools like DBUnit, but is much simpler, and focuses on a single task: populate the database with test data."*

- Github
- Documentation
- Download
- JavaDoc
- Maven artifact

```
<dependency>
    <groupId>com.ninja-squad</groupId>
    <artifactId>DbSetup</artifactId>
    <version>1.2.0</version>
    <scope>test</scope>
</dependency>
```

Fongo

> *"Fongo is an in-memory java implementation of mongo. It intercepts calls to the standard mongo-java-driver for finds, updates, inserts, removes and other methods. The primary use is for lightweight unit testing where you don't want to spin up a mongo process."*

- Github
- Maven artifact

```
<dependency>
    <groupId>com.github.fakemongo</groupId>
    <artifactId>fongo</artifactId>
    <version>1.4.4</version>
    <scope>test</scope>
</dependency>
```

Greenmail

"GreenMail is an open source, intuitive and easy-to-use test suite of email servers for testing purposes. Supports SMTP, POP3, IMAP with SSL socket support. GreenMail also provides a JBoss GreenMail Service."

- Sourceforge
- Documentation
- Download
- JavaDoc
- Maven artifact

```
<dependency>
    <groupId>com.icegreen</groupId>
    <artifactId>greenmail</artifactId>
    <version>1.3.1b</version>
    <scope>test</scope>
</dependency>
```

Dumbster

"The Dumbster is a very simple fake SMTP server designed for unit and system testing applications that send email messages. It responds to all standard SMTP commands but does not deliver messages to the user. The messages are stored within the Dumbster for later extraction and verification."

- Sourceforge
- Documentation
- Download
- JavaDoc
- Maven artifact

```
<dependency>
    <groupId>dumbster</groupId>
    <artifactId>dumbster</artifactId>
    <version>1.6</version>
    <scope>test</scope>
</dependency>
```

MockFtpServer

"The MockFtpServer project provides a mock/dummy FTP server implementations that can be very useful for testing of FTP client code. Two FTP Server implementations are provided, each at a different level of abstraction."

- Sourceforge

- Documentation
- Download
- JavaDoc
- Maven artifact

```xml
<dependency>
    <groupId>org.mockftpserver</groupId>
    <artifactId>MockFtpServer</artifactId>
    <version>2.4</version>
    <scope>test</scope>
</dependency>
```

In-container related frameworks

Spring Test

- GitHub
- Documentation
- Download
- JavaDoc
- Maven artifact

```
<dependency>
    <groupId>org.springframework</groupId>
    <artifactId>spring-framework-bom</artifactId>
    <version>4.0.5.RELEASE</version>
    <type>pom</type>
    <scope>import</scope>
</dependency>
<dependency>
    <groupId>org.springframework</groupId>
    <artifactId>spring-test</artifactId>
    <scope>test</scope>
</dependency>
```

Springockito

"This is a small extension to spring that simplifies way of creation mockito mocks in the intergation tests' related context xml files."

- Bitbucket
- Documentation
- Maven artifact

```
<dependency>
    <groupId>org.kubek2k</groupId>
    <artifactId>springockito</artifactId>
    <version>1.0.9</version>
    <scope>test</scope>
</dependency>
```

Arquillian

"Arquillian is an innovative and highly extensible testing platform for the JVM that enables developers to easily create automated integration, functional and acceptance tests for Java middleware."

- Github
- Documentation
- Maven artifact

```xml
<dependency>
    <groupId>org.jboss.arquillian</groupId>
    <artifactId>arquillian-bom</artifactId>
    <version>1.1.5.Final</version>
    <type>pom</type>
    <scope>import</scope>
</dependency>
<dependency>
    <groupId>org.jboss.arquillian.testng</groupId>
    <artifactId>arquillian-testng-container</artifactId>
    <scope>test</scope>
</dependency>
```

Tomcat DBCP

"The JDBC Connection Pool `org.apache.tomcat.jdbc.pool` is a replace-ment or an alternative to the Apache Commons DBCP connection pool."

- Apache SVN
- Download (but all Tomcat must be downloaded)
- Documentation
- JavaDocs (includes all of Tomcat's JavaDocs)
- Maven artifact

```
<dependency>
    <groupId>org.apache.tomcat</groupId>
    <artifactId>tomcat-jdbc</artifactId>
    <version>7.0.35</version>
    <scope>test</scope>
</dependency>
```

C3P0

"c3p0 is an easy-to-use library for making traditional JDBC drivers "enterprise-ready" by augmenting them with functionality defined by the jdbc3 spec and the optional extensions to jdbc2. In particular, c3p0 provides several useful services:

- *Classes which adapt traditional DriverManager-based JDBC drivers to the newer javax.sql.DataSource scheme for acquiring database Connections.*

> • *Transparent pooling of Connection and PreparedStatements behind DataSources which can "wrap" around traditional drivers or arbitrary unpooled DataSources."*

- Github
- Download
- Documentation
- JavaDocs
- Maven artifact

```xml
<dependency>
    <groupId>com.mchange</groupId>
    <artifactId>c3p0</artifactId>
    <version>0.9.2.1</version>
    <scope>test</scope>
</dependency>
```

Miscellaneous libraries

Joda Time

> *"Joda-Time provides a quality replacement for the Java date and time classes. The design allows for multiple calendar systems, while still providing a simple API. The 'default' calendar is the ISO8601 standard which is used by XML. The Gregorian, Julian, Buddhist, Coptic, Ethiopic and Islamic systems are also included, and we welcome further additions. Supporting classes include time zone, duration, format and parsing."*

- Github
- Download
- Documentation
- JavaDocs
- Maven artifact

```
<dependency>
    <groupId>joda-time</groupId>
    <artifactId>joda-time</artifactId>
    <version>2.3</version>
</dependency>
```

Spark

"A Sinatra inspired micro web framework for quickly creating web applications in Java with minimal effort"

- Github
- Download
- Documentation*
- Maven artifacts

```
<dependency>
    <groupId>com.sparkjava</groupId>
    <artifactId>spark-core</artifactId>
    <version>1.1.1</version>
    <scope>test</scope>
</dependency>
<dependency>
    <groupId>com.sparkjava</groupId>
        <artifactId>spark-template-velocity</artifactId>
    <version>1.0</version>
    <scope>test</scope>
</dependency>
```

```
<dependency>
    <groupId>com.sparkjava</groupId>
        <artifactId>spark-template-freemarker</artifactId>
    <version>1.0</version>
    <scope>test</scope>
</dependency>
```

SoapUI

"SoapUI is a free and open source cross-platform Functional Testing solution."

- Github
- Download
- Documentation
- JavaDocs
- Maven artifacts

```xml
<dependency>
    <groupId>com.smartbear.soapui</groupId>
    <artifactId>soapui</artifactId>
    <version>5.0.0</version>
    <scope>test</scope>
</dependency>

<!-- SoapUI is not on Maven Central -->
<repository>
    <id>soapui</id>
    <url>http://www.soapui.org/repository/maven2/</url>
</repository>
```

Made in the USA
San Bernardino, CA
27 February 2017